TO: MARION

# VIEWER RAVES

"Thank you for such a fun and wonderful cooking show. I have watched and enjoyed cooking shows for many years but none have managed to get me in the kitchen and rattle those pots and pans. Your show has released a frustrated cook."

*Gloria*
Nanaimo, B.C.

"I'm an avid fan of your show *What's for Dinner?* Your recipes and accompanying tips have left my family and friends surprised by my culinary abilities."

*Maria*
Mississauga, Ont.

"I love your show and watch it religiously. I think that your recipes are simple to prepare, ingredients easy to acquire and the results excellent!"

*Michael*
St. John's, Nfld.

"I want to thank you so much for giving me such confidence in the kitchen. You are a pleasure to watch. Keep up the good work."

*Alda*
Winnipeg, Man.

"My husband and I both enjoy your show. We especially like the fact that you have a lot of vegetarian meals and that your meals are light."

*Jaqui*
Dollard des Ormeaux, Que.

# What's for Dinner?

# What's for Dinner?

## KEN KOSTICK

*Macmillan Canada*
*Toronto*

Canadian Cataloguing in Publication Data

Kostick, Ken,    1953–
        What's for Dinner?

Includes index.
ISBN 0–7715–7372–3

1. Dinners and dining. 2. Cookery. 3. Quick and easy cookery. 4. Low-calorie diet – Recipes. I. Title

TX737.K67 1996       641.5'4       C95–932613–8

Macmillan Canada wishes to thank the Canada Council, the Ontario Arts Council and the Ontario Ministry of Culture and Communications for supporting its publishing program.

Macmillan Canada
A Division of Canada Publishing Corporation
Toronto, Canada

Cover and inside design:    Stray Toaster
Front-cover photo:    David Hlynsky
Back-cover and photo on page i:    Christoph Strube
Photo on page 176: George Nanos
Composition:    IBEX Graphic Communications Inc.

1 2 3 4 5      00 99 98 97 96

Printed in Canada

To my parents, Ed and Helen,  my initial cooking knowledge and taught me how <obscured> d is in the world.

I know if my father were here <obscured> be proud.

Much love, and thank yo<obscured>

I love your show *What's for Dinner?* I think it's the best cooking show I've ever seen on television.

I love all your recipes—they're fun, healthy and easy for an amateur like myself…. One can tell you really enjoy cooking and it's given me more incentive to cook.

My husband and I are the parents of four young children and would love seeing some recipes on the show that would be appropriate for larger families with young children. I'm sure you probably have done some recipes of that nature but I might have missed them.

Thank you for such a wonderful show! I love your dog Ken. She's a sweetheart.

Yours truly,

*Karen*
Kanata, Ont.

# CONTENTS

# ACKNOWLEDGMENTS

I would like to thank a few people who helped and inspired me to do this book—and the TV show:

Shaine Jaffe—my agent who always gives me the right advice.

Ira Levy and Peter Williamson, of The Friendly Kitchen Company, who believed in my recipes—and in me.

Laura, Carolyn, Tania, Sandra, Suzanne, Emily and Mike—all of The Friendly Kitchen Company.

Life Network, who envisioned a cooking show called *What's for Dinner?* and who had confidence in my recipes.

The television crew of *What's for Dinner?*

Macmillan Canada—Denise Schon and Nicole de Montbrun, who from day one encouraged me to do this cookbook.

Anne Smyth and Pauline Hanson, who assisted me in testing all the recipes.

Donald Martin, who always encouraged me to take the recipes out of my head and put them on paper.

Gil Humphreys, who tried a majority of the recipes and gave me constructive feedback.

My sister Diane and friends Bob, Barry, Brian, Craig, Nancy and Doug, who were all great tasters.

Jamie Hanson, who has given me the support and daily advice to finish this cookbook.

Ruby, my dog, who was there with that cute face every day.

And Pearl, my new boxer, who just wants me to cuddle her.

To the chefs who always know what's for dinner:

Having to cook meals and prepare snacks all day for my diabetic two-year-old can get monotonous and frustrating, at times. As you know, two-year-olds really don't have the time to stop and eat, and they become fussy when you force the issue. As luck would have it, my daughter has a real taste for food, and the hints and substitutions in your quick and easy recipes have helped tremendously.

I want to say thank you for helping me keep the taste in what would have been a dull diabetic diet.

Now, I *always* know what's for dinner!


Yours truly,


*Debbie & Chelsey*
Bolton, Ont.

# INTRODUCTION

All of my most wonderful memories are of food and cooking.

My love of cooking and knowledge of food comes not only from traveling the world sampling a wide array of dishes but also from parents who were excellent cooks.

When I was growing up in Winnipeg, cooking duties were shared by my parents: my mother, Helen, would prepare the meals during the week; my father, Ed, on weekends. They encouraged my sister Diane and me to cook and to experiment at an early age. I prepared my first meal at the age of six: it was a modest mélange of scrambled eggs with ketchup and wieners—as my mother remembers it, the wieners were not quite al dente.

The kitchen was the center of our world: we both congregated and entertained guests there. All important decisions were made there, too.

It was in my parents' kitchen that I learned to be inventive with leftovers. My parents had little money, but were forced to be innovative with food because sometimes there were as many as seven children to feed. Besides my sister Diane and me, there were our foster brothers and sisters of all ages who needed good, nourishing meals. (To this day, these grown "foster children" still visit and call my mother "Mom.") As well, my parents were always feeding elderly, lonely or homeless people food they had prepared.

It was my parents who influenced and inspired me to be adventurous, to feel comfortable creating recipes, to host dinner parties of ten and more, and to write this cookbook.

## THE TV SHOW

*What's for Dinner?* has been a thrill for me, even though, before this, I never aspired, nor thought I would want, to host a cooking show. From its inception, and as an associate producer, my only intention was to contribute recipes and work closely on the concept with The Friendly Kitchen Company and Life Network.

We were lucky enough, after six weeks of looking for a host, to stumble upon Mary Jo Eustace, a talented singer, model and sous-chef.

But, just three weeks before we were to begin shooting, and after many auditions, the executive producers still hadn't found the right co-host for Mary Jo.

That's when they approached me.

I remember thinking at the time: I've never done television! What if I'm terrible at it? Voicing this concern elicited the comment: "Well, we'll just have to fire you then."

I thought: Okay, I'll try it! And then jumped right in.

During the first season, we shot 110 half-hour episodes of *What's for Dinner?* It aired five days a week, four times a day on Life Network and garnered a loyal and burgeoning viewership of all ages, whose members soon began sending, and, continue to send in a surprising number of letters (some of which are excerpted here).

Working with Mary Jo has been fun. Like me, she has a wacky sense of humor and, as our on-air relationship has evolved, this wackiness and our banter has led some viewers to express their concern. This is just to reassure them: we're really not bickering! It's just our unusual brand of back-and-forth.

One important aspect of our show is that all the cooking is done in real time. Every recipe, from start to finish, takes at most a half hour, and, every aspect of the dish is prepared on air. This, of course, has led to some tense moments but, in the end, the uncertainty has only added to the fun.

Since the show began, I have made many references to my mother Helen (and her bingo friends) and to my boxer Ruby. As well, Ruby's portrait adorns the refrigerator on the set, and my mother has appeared on the show to prepare her famous perogies. All this media attention has nearly made them celebrities. Well, there's been a new addition to my family—the adorable, white boxer Pearl (see back cover) is now poised to make *her* debut!

## THE COOKBOOK

About three years ago—two years before the idea of a television show was being kicked around—I began writing this cookbook. The idea occurred to me while on a flight to one of the many destinations my other job (as a scout for a Milan-based modeling agency) takes me. The concept was simple: easy, delicious recipes that could be ready in a half hour.

Within this cookbook, you'll find a glossary of terms, tips and cooking methods, a detailed index to the recipes and their ingredients, and an address at which you can write to me.

Many variations and substitutions are suggested alongside the recipes so that you can do what I do and experiment: if you don't have fresh basil, use dried basil; if you can't get fennel, use celery; if you don't have veal, substitute chicken or fish. Use what you have and use my recipes only as guidelines, if you wish.

There are also low-fat options for almost all the recipes. When I cook for myself, I try to use as little fat as possible. In the past two years, I have lost a whopping 60 pounds thanks to a combination of low-fat healthy cooking and exercise (I run 10 to 15 kilometers a day and am training to run in a marathon).

My message for you as you use this book is: have fun, don't panic, involve your friends and family, and do it all in 30 minutes!

I would like to say that I really enjoy your show and watch it whenever I can. In Winnipeg, it is on every night at 10:00 p.m. and I now watch it instead of *Murphy Brown*.

I especially like:

- that it is a Canadian show;

- the format of making a complete meal in approximately a half hour;

- the recipes are economical and the ingredients are what most of us have on hand;

- good suggestions given for substitutions;

- your recipes are very healthy and have a low-fat content; and

- it is fun to listen to the chitchat between you both about your dogs, your family, etc.

I enjoyed when Ken's mother visited to make perogies.

Keep up the good work!

Sincerely,

*Joyce*
Winnipeg, Man.

# APPETIZERS, SOUPS AND SALADS

# BRUSCHETTA
*Serves 4–6.*

This is a typical starter in Europe, but I like to serve bruschetta as a side dish at lunch with a soup.

| | |
|---|---|
| 1 loaf | French bread |
| 4 | small tomatoes, chopped |
| 2 cloves | garlic, minced |
| 1/2 cup | chopped fresh basil |
| 1 tsp | lemon juice |
| 1 tbsp | olive oil |
| 1 tsp | balsamic vinegar |
| 1 tsp | black pepper |
| 1/4 cup | grated Parmesan cheese |

Slice the bread lengthwise and toast. In a bowl, mix together the tomatoes, garlic, basil, lemon juice, oil, balsamic vinegar and pepper. Spread tomato mixture over the toasted bread and sprinkle with Parmesan cheese. Broil for 2–3 minutes until cheese has melted.

**PREPARATION TIME:** *15–25 minutes*

VARIATIONS:
- For individuals who have wheat allergies, use spelt or rice-flour bread.
- You can replace the tomatoes with chopped zucchini.

# ROASTED CHICKEN FINGERS
*Serves 4.*

Mary Jo and I did this healthy recipe on our "Kids' Show." It was a lot of fun.

| | |
|---|---|
| 2 | boneless skinless chicken breasts |
| 1/4 cup | dry bread crumbs |
| 1/4 cup | all-purpose flour |
| 1 tsp | garlic powder |
| 1 tbsp | paprika |
| 1/2 tsp | salt |
| 1/2 tsp | black pepper |
| 1 | egg, beaten |

Slice chicken into strips. Mix together the bread crumbs, flour, garlic powder, paprika, salt and pepper. Dip chicken strips in egg, then into bread crumb mixture. Arrange on greased or nonstick baking sheet. Bake at 425°F for 15–20 minutes, turning occasionally, till golden and crispy.

**PREPARATION TIME:**     *10 minutes*

VARIATIONS:
- Replace the chicken with turkey.
- Replace the bread crumbs with crushed corn flakes or crisp rice cereal.

# TAPAS

*Serves 6.*

The "Tapas Show" was one of the crew's favorites. Ten minutes after we stopped taping, everything edible had been eaten. Tapas—a selection of various dishes combining seafood, poultry, vegetables and rice—is a very common meal in Spain.

### JUMBO SHRIMP IN GARLIC:

| | |
|---|---|
| 8 | jumbo shrimp |
| 2 tbsp | olive oil |
| 4 cloves | garlic, minced |
| 2 | small shallots, chopped |
| 1 tsp | fresh thyme |

SUGGESTED SIDE DISHES:
- Saffron rice with raisins
- Garlic and Potato Soup with Tomatoes (recipe on p. 12)

Peel and devein shrimp, leaving tails on. In a large skillet, sauté, put in casserole and bake at 350°F for 5–10 minutes.

### PAN-FRIED SQUID WITH LEMON AND FENNEL:

| | |
|---|---|
| 2 cups | sliced squid |
| 2 tbsp | olive oil |
| | Juice and pulp of 1 lemon |
| 1/4 cup | chopped fennel |
| 1 tsp | lemon zest |
| 1 tsp | dried parsley |
| 1/2 cup | chopped spinach |

Sauté, put in casserole and bake at 350°F for 5–10 minutes.

### CHICKEN WITH TOMATOES AND BASIL:

| | |
|---|---|
| 2 | boneless skinless chicken breasts |
| 1 tsp | olive oil |
| 1/4 cup | chopped fresh basil |
| 2 | plum tomatoes, chopped |
| 1/4 cup | red wine |
| | Salt and black pepper to taste |

Sauté, put in casserole and bake at 350°F for 5–10 minutes.

# TAPAS

*continued*

### VEGETABLES BAKED IN HERBS:

| | |
|---|---|
| 1/2 | zucchini, sliced |
| 1 | small onion, chopped |
| 1 | potato, sliced |
| 2 | carrots, sliced |
| 1/2 cup | cubed eggplant |
| 2 | plum tomatoes, chopped |
| 1/2 cup | broccoli florets |
| 1/2 cup | cauliflower florets |
| 1/2 tsp | dried basil |
| 1/2 tsp | dried oregano |
| 1/2 tsp | dried rosemary |
| | Salt and black pepper to taste |

Sauté, place in casserole and bake at 350°F for 5–10 minutes.

### MUSHROOMS, GARLIC AND ONIONS:

| | |
|---|---|
| 2 cups | chopped mushrooms |
| 1 | small onion, chopped |
| 2 cloves | garlic, minced |
| 1 tbsp | olive oil |
| | Salt and black pepper to taste |

Put in casserole and bake at 350°F for 10–15 minutes.

**PREPARATION TIME:**    *30–35 minutes*

**TIME SAVER:**

Tapas makes great party food. Sauté the tapas the day before and bake the day of the party.

VARIATION:
— Replace saffron in the side dish with curry, turmeric or cumin.

LOW-FAT OPTION:
— Replace most of the oil with soup stock or juice; be aware, though, that this will change the texture *and* flavor.

# GOAT CHEESE AND HERB OMELETTE

*Serves 4–6 as appetizer.*

I made this on the "Egg Show." Egg dishes are very economical and quick dinners. Invent other variations to suit your taste.

| | |
|---|---|
| 4–6 | eggs |
| 1/4 cup | table cream or milk |
| 1/2 tsp | dried rosemary |
| 1/2 tsp | dried basil |
| 1 tbsp | butter |
| 1/4 tsp | salt |
| 1/4 tsp | black pepper |
| 1/4 cup | chopped pitted black olives |
| 1/2 cup | soft goat cheese |
| | Fresh rosemary sprigs and sliced goat cheese for garnish |

In a bowl, mix together the eggs, cream, herbs, salt and pepper. In a nonstick sauté pan, melt butter over medium heat. Pour in egg mixture; slide spatula under the egg mixture to allow uncooked egg to run underneath. When egg mixture is just about firm, flip the omelette over and arrange the olives and goat cheese in the center. Fold the omelette in half. Slice into wedges and garnish with rosemary and cheese.

**PREPARATION TIME:**     *15–20 minutes*

VARIATION:
— Replace cheese with soft tofu.

LOW-FAT OPTION:
— Replace the cream or milk with low-fat sour cream or non-fat yogurt.

# FRITTATA
*Serves 4–6 as appetizer.*

A frittata uses the same ingredients as an omelette, but the filling is blended with the egg mixture. Frittatas make great brunch or dinner entrées.

| | |
|---|---|
| 1 | small onion, chopped |
| 1 clove | garlic, minced |
| 1 tbsp | butter |
| 1 tsp | oil |
| 6 | eggs |
| 1/4 cup | table or half-and-half cream |
| 1/2 cup | chopped sweet red pepper |
| 1/2 cup | chopped mushrooms |
| 1/4 cup | grated Parmesan cheese |
| 1/4 tsp | paprika |
| | Selection of chopped herbs such as rosemary, thyme, chives |

In a medium skillet, sauté the onions and garlic in butter and oil until translucent. Meanwhile, in a bowl, mix the eggs, cream, red pepper, mushrooms, Parmesan cheese, paprika and herbs. Pour the egg mixture into the skillet; reduce heat to medium. As frittata sets, use a spatula to lift the frittata to allow the uncooked egg to run underneath. Put a plate on the top to flatten the frittata. Cook 6–8 minutes, checking to make sure the bottom does not burn. Flip the frittata onto a plate.

**PREPARATION TIME:**     *12–15 minutes*

LOW-FAT OPTIONS:
— Replace the cream with low-fat sour cream.
— Replace the butter with calorie-reduced margarine.

# SUMMER CITY VEGETABLE SOUP
### Serves 4–6.

This soup's name was inspired by the abundance of fresh vegetables in the summer, when I first prepared it. Don't be scared off by the number of ingredients; just sharpen that knife and get chopping.

| | |
|---|---|
| 1 | medium onion, chopped |
| 2 | celery stalks, chopped |
| 2 | boiling potatoes, diced |
| 1/2 cup | diced carrots |
| 1 tbsp | olive oil |
| 3 cloves | garlic, chopped |
| 1 can | tomatoes with juice (28 oz/796 mL) |
| 1/2 tsp | salt |
| 1 tsp | black pepper |
| 1 tsp | hot sauce |
| 1 | bay leaf |
| 1/2 cup | chopped fresh basil |
| 1 | small zucchini, chopped |
| 1/2 cup | chopped sweet red or yellow pepper |
| 1/2 cup | chopped cabbage |
| 3 cups | water |

**SUGGESTED SIDE DISHES:**
- Grilled vegetables on fresh Italian bread
- Radicchio salad with tomatoes and leaf lettuce

In a crock pot or large heavy saucepan, gently sauté the onion, celery, potatoes and carrots in oil for about 3 minutes. Add the garlic and sauté another 2 minutes. Raise the heat to high and add the tomatoes, salt, pepper, hot sauce, bay leaf, basil, zucchini, peppers, cabbage and water. Bring to a boil; reduce heat to simmer, uncovered, 15–20 minutes. If the liquid evaporates, add more water. Soup is ready to serve when harder vegetables are tender. Discard the bay leaf before serving.

**PREPARATION TIME:**     *25–30 minutes*

**TIME SAVER:**

Chop some of the vegetables and herbs together in a food processor. Cube potatoes and carrots so they will cook more quickly.

VARIATION:
— Replace any of the vegetables with others you might have left over.

LOW-FAT OPTION:
— Use a nonstick pot and leave out the oil.

# CHICKEN RICE SOUP WITH LEMON

*Serves 4–6.*

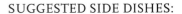

This is one way to be creative with leftovers. Try to find canned or powdered chicken broth without salt and MSG.

| | |
|---|---|
| 1 | lemon |
| 2 cups | chicken broth |
| 2 cups | water |
| 1 | medium onion, chopped |
| 1/4 cup | chopped fresh basil |
| 1/2 cup | chopped celery |
| 1/2 cup | uncooked rice OR |
| | 1 cup cooked rice |
| 1 | bay leaf |
| 1/2 tsp | salt |
| 1/2 tsp | black pepper |
| 1/2 tsp | dried oregano |
| 1/4 tsp | dried sage |
| | Chicken bones (optional) |
| 2 | carrots, chopped |
| 2 | tomatoes, chopped |
| 1 cup | chopped cooked chicken |
| 1/4 cup | grated Parmesan cheese |

**SUGGESTED SIDE DISHES:**

- Lentil salad
- Grilled cheddar cheese on French bread
- Cucumber salad

Cut the lemon in half. Thinly slice one half; put aside. Remove 1/2 tsp zest from second half; put aside. Reserve juice from second half. In a heavy saucepan, combine the lemon juice, chicken stock, water, onion, basil, celery, uncooked rice (if using), bay leaf, salt, pepper, oregano, sage and chicken bones (if using). Bring to a boil, reduce heat and simmer, uncovered, 15–20 minutes. Remove bones. Add lemon slices, cooked rice (if using), carrots and tomatoes. Simmer another 5 minutes. Stir in the cooked chicken and simmer for 5 minutes. Discard the bay leaf. Add lemon zest and Parmesan cheese to garnish.

**PREPARATION TIME:**     *25–30 minutes*

VARIATION:
- For a vegetarian dish, replace the chicken with tofu.

# TURKEY SOUP WITH VEGETABLES AND PASTA

*Serves 4–6.*

My mother, Helen (who prepared her perogies on the show) taught me this variation of turkey soup. This quick and economical soup became a family favorite. There is only one gram of fat per ounce of turkey meat; turkey is also a source of protein, B vitamins and iron.

| | |
|---|---|
| 2 tbsp | olive or vegetable oil |
| 1 | small onion, chopped |
| 1/2 cup | shredded carrot |
| 1/2 cup | chopped celery |
| 1 can | crushed or stewed tomatoes (19 oz/540 mL) |
| 4 cups | water |
| 1/4 cup | chopped fresh basil (or 1/2 tsp dried) |
| 1 tbsp | chopped fresh tarragon (or 1/2 tsp dry) |
| 1 tbsp | chopped fresh sage (or 1/4 tsp dried) |
| 1 | bay leaf |
| 1/2 tsp | sea salt |
| 1/2 tsp | black pepper |
| 2 cups | chopped cooked turkey |
| 1/2 cup | uncooked macaroni or other small pasta shape |
| | Fresh sage or parsley sprigs and grated Parmesan cheese for garnish |

SUGGESTED SIDE DISHES:
- Assortment of open-faced sandwiches
- Bruschetta (recipe on p. 2)

In a crock pot or large heavy saucepan, heat the oil. Sauté the onions, carrots and celery for 2–3 minutes. Add the tomatoes, water, basil, tarragon, sage, bay leaf, salt and pepper. Simmer, covered, 10 minutes. Add cooked turkey. Simmer, covered, another 10 minutes. If liquid reduces too much, add a little water or tomato juice. Add pasta. Simmer, uncovered and stirring occasionally, another 8–10 minutes until pasta is cooked. Discard the bay leaf. Ladle soup into bowls and garnish with fresh sprigs of sage or parsley and a sprinkle of Parmesan cheese, if desired.

# TURKEY SOUP WITH VEGETABLES AND PASTA
*continued*

**PREPARATION TIME:**     *25–30 minutes*

**TIME SAVER:**
Use a food processor to chop and shred vegetables.
Use fresh pasta, or cook pasta separately while soup
is cooking. Stir drained pasta into soup and serve
immediately.

VARIATIONS:
- Replace crushed tomatoes with another vegetable or chicken stock.
- Replace pasta with uncooked rice.

LOW-FAT OPTION:
- Leave out the oil and make the soup in a nonstick saucepan.

# GARLIC AND POTATO SOUP WITH TOMATOES

*Serves 6.*

The "Soup Show" was a big favorite of our viewers. We received a lot of letters telling us they loved the different soups as a dinner. Homemade soups really can be made within 30 minutes—just use your imagination. When making your own soups, choose canned tomatoes and soup stocks that are low in sodium and contain no MSG.

| | |
|---|---|
| 1 | large onion, chopped |
| 3 cloves | garlic, minced |
| 1 tbsp | olive oil |
| 1 can | crushed tomatoes (28 oz/796 mL) |
| 1 tsp | tomato paste |
| 1/4 cup | chopped fresh basil |
| 1/4 cup | chopped fresh dill |
| 1 | bay leaf |
| 2 cups | vegetable stock |
| 1/2 tsp | salt |
| 1/2 tsp | black pepper |
| 2 cups | mashed potatoes |

SUGGESTED SIDE DISHES:
- Green salad
- Italian herbed bread
- Calabrese bread

In a large heavy saucepan, sauté onions and garlic in olive oil until translucent. Add the tomatoes, tomato paste, basil, dill, bay leaf, vegetable stock, salt and pepper. Simmer 15–20 minutes. Discard the bay leaf. Stir in the mashed potatoes. Using a hand blender, purée the soup in the pot (or purée in batches in a food processor).

**PREPARATION TIME:** *20–25 minutes*

# CREAM OF TOMATO SOUP WITH NON-FAT YOGURT

*Serves 6.*

I love the flavor of cream soups, but I must say that since losing weight (60 lb) I try to limit my fat intake. Therefore I purée a lot and use non-fat yogurt or low-fat sour cream to get the creamy texture. Try some of these variations.

| | |
|---|---|
| 1 | large onion, chopped |
| 1 clove | garlic, minced |
| 1 tbsp | olive oil |
| 1 can | stewed tomatoes (28 oz/796 mL) |
| 1 tbsp | tomato paste |
| 1/4 cup | chopped parsley |
| 2 cups | vegetable stock |
| 1 | bay leaf |
| 1/2 tsp | dried basil |
| 1/2 tsp | dried oregano |
| 1/4 tsp | chili powder |
| 1/2 tsp | salt |
| 1/2 tsp | black pepper |
| 1 cup | non-fat yogurt or low-fat sour cream |
| 1/2 cup | chopped watercress for garnish |

SUGGESTED SIDE DISHES:
- Green salad
- Italian herbed bread
- Calabrese bread

In a large heavy saucepan, sauté the onion and garlic in oil until translucent. Add tomatoes, tomato paste, parsley, vegetable stock, bay leaf, basil oregano, chili powder, salt and pepper; bring to a boil. Reduce heat and simmer, uncovered and stirring occasionally, about 20 minutes. Discard the bay leaf. Add the yogurt and mix gently. Garnish with watercress.

**PREPARATION TIME:** *20–25 minutes*

# CURRIED CHICKEN AND EGG SOUP

*Serves 6.*

I love soups and the different flavors you can create with spices. Curry is one of my favorites. I first had a variation of this soup in the Middle East years ago. I used to order it every day for lunch with a pita bread sandwich. Explore with your taste buds.

| | |
|---|---|
| 1 | small onion, chopped |
| 2 cloves | garlic, minced |
| 1 tsp | olive oil |
| 4 | celery stalks, chopped |
| 2 | large carrots, chopped |
| 3 cups | chicken stock |
| 1/4 cup | chopped fresh coriander |
| 1/4 cup | chopped parsley |
| 1 tsp | mild curry paste |
| 1 tsp | Worcestershire sauce |
| 1 | bay leaf |
| 1/2 tsp | salt |
| 1/2 tsp | black pepper |
| 1 cup | chopped cooked chicken |
| 1/2 cup | cooked or frozen peas |
| 2 | eggs |
| 1/2 cup | non-fat yogurt for garnish |

SUGGESTED SIDE DISHES:
- Green salad
- Italian herbed bread
- Calabrese bread

In a large heavy saucepan, sauté onion and garlic in oil until translucent. Add the celery and carrots and sauté another 2 minutes. Add chicken stock, coriander, parsley, curry paste, Worcestershire sauce, bay leaf, salt and pepper. Simmer, uncovered, 10–15 minutes until vegetables are tender. Add chicken and peas and simmer another 5 minutes. Discard the bay leaf. Break eggs into soup and mix gently. Ladle into bowls and top with a tablespoon of yogurt.

**PREPARATION TIME:**     *20–25 minutes*

VARIATION:
Replace chicken with turkey.

# CAULIFLOWER AND BLUE CHEESE SOUP

*Serves 4–6.*

On "What's for Dinner?" I love to make soups. At home I make several versions of each soup and experiment with various ingredients. The following two soups are a couple of my favorites, and I serve them as a main meal, as they are so rich and creamy.

| | |
|---|---|
| 2 tbsp | olive oil |
| 1 | medium onion, chopped |
| 2 cups | vegetable stock |
| 1 | large cauliflower, chopped |
| 1/4 cup | chopped fresh dill |
| 1/4 cup | chopped fresh chives |
| 1 | bay leaf |
| 1/4 tsp | salt |
| 1/2 tsp | black pepper |
| 2 | egg yolks |
| 1 cup | whipping cream |
| 1 cup | crumbled blue cheese |
| 2 cups | milk |

SUGGESTED SIDE DISH:
- Bread toasted with watercress and goat cheese

In a large heavy saucepan, heat oil. Sauté onion for 1 minute; add vegetable stock. Bring to boil. Meanwhile, microwave the cauliflower, covered, at High for 1 minute. Add cauliflower to soup; reduce heat and simmer 10 minutes. Stir in half the dill, half the chives, bay leaf, salt and pepper. Mix the egg yolks with the cream; stir into the soup. Stir in the blue cheese and milk. Simmer another 10 minutes; do not let the soup boil. Discard the bay leaf. Using a hand blender or food processor, purée the soup. Stir in the remaining dill and chives and serve immediately.

**PREPARATION TIME:**     *20–25 minutes*

TIP:

➤ Replace the vegetable stock with non-fat chicken stock. You can buy chicken stock that has no preservatives and is low in fat and sodium. Make sure when cooking with creams and cheeses not to boil or burn the soup.

LOW-FAT OPTIONS:

— Replace whipping cream with milk or low-fat sour cream.

— Replace milk with a non-fat milk beverage or skim milk.

# CREAM OF MUSHROOM SOUP

*Serves 4–6.*

| | |
|---|---|
| 1 tbsp | olive oil |
| 2 | shallots (or 1 small onion), chopped |
| 1 clove | garlic, minced |
| 4 cups | finely chopped mushrooms |
| 2 cups | vegetable stock |
| 1/4 cup | all-purpose flour |
| 1/4 cup | chopped parsley |
| 1/2 tsp | dried basil |
| 1/4 tsp | salt |
| 1/2 tsp | black pepper |
| 1 tbsp | lemon juice |
| 1 cup | milk |
| 1/2 cup | non-fat yogurt or low-fat sour cream |
| 1 cup | half-and-half cream |
| 1/2 cup | whipping cream |
| | Parsley or watercress for garnish |

In a large heavy saucepan, heat oil. Sauté shallots and garlic until translucent. Add the mushrooms and sauté until browned. Add the vegetable stock. Stir in the flour while heating. Add the parsley, basil, salt, pepper and lemon juice. Bring to a boil; reduce heat to simmer 15 minutes. Add the milk, yogurt, half-and-half cream and whipping cream. Heat through. Ladle soup into bowls and garnish with parsley or watercress.

**PREPARATION TIME:**    *20–25 minutes*

SUGGESTED SIDE DISHES:
- Bread toasted with watercress and goat cheese
- Tossed salad with meat or cheese and oil-and-vinegar dressing

TIPS:
- This soup can be thickened with cream or a flour-and-water mixture and used as a sauce.
- Replace the vegetable stock with non-fat chicken stock. You can buy chicken stock that has no preservatives and is low in fat and sodium.
- Increase the amount of non-fat yogurt and replace cream and whipping cream with soy milk or water. Before you add water, purée the mushrooms to give a creamy texture.

VARIATIONS:
- Use fresh dill instead of parsley.
- Replace or add other vegetables that you have left over.

LOW-FAT OPTIONS:
- Replace whipping cream with low-fat sour cream.
- Replace milk with a non-fat milk beverage or skim milk.

# Very Creamy Clam Chowder with Crab

*Serves 4–6.*

We are talking *very creamy*. This chowder is a wonderful main course, served with grilled vegetables and a hearty bread or bruschetta. On the East Coast this is called just "The Soup."

| | |
|---|---|
| 1 tbsp | olive oil |
| 1/2 cup | diced potato |
| 1/2 cup | chopped onion |
| 1/2 cup | chopped sweet red pepper |
| 1/2 cup | water |
| 1 cup | fresh or canned (rinsed) clams |
| 1/2 cup | crab meat |
| 1/2 cup | chopped fresh dill |
| 1 cup | table cream |
| 1 cup | milk |
| 1/2 tsp | salt |
| 1 tsp | black pepper |
| 1/2 cup | shredded cheddar cheese |

SUGGESTED SIDE DISHES:
- Warm bruschetta with basil and goat cheese
- Assortment of grilled vegetables

In a crock pot or heavy saucepan, heat the oil. Sauté the potato and onion for 3 minutes. Add the red pepper and sauté for another minute. Bring to a boil and add the water. Reduce heat and simmer for 2 minutes. Add the clams and crab meat; simmer another 5 minutes. Add half the dill, the cream, milk, salt, pepper and half the cheddar cheese. Reduce heat and simmer for another 15 minutes, gently stirring. Make sure the soup does not boil. Ladle into bowls and garnish with the remaining dill and cheese.

**PREPARATION TIME:**     *20–25 minutes*

**TIME SAVER:**
Microwave potatoes while chopping other vegetables.

TIP:
If you are making this chowder for the kids, it's probably a good idea to substitute non-fat yogurt for cream. It's been shown that children who eat yogurt have greater resistance to flu infections.

VARIATION:
Replace seafood with mushrooms and other vegetables.

LOW-FAT OPTIONS:
Replace cream with low-fat sour cream.
Replace milk with non-fat milk beverage or skim milk.
Replace cheese with low-fat cheese substitute.

# FRUITY STRAWBERRY SALAD
### Serves 3–4.

Mary Jo and I prepared the following three salads on the "Salad Show"; viewer mail poured in with variations on the three dressings. Experiment with different types of lettuce: leaf, romaine, boston, radicchio and—the most common—iceberg. You can add whatever you want to the salad, but plain is just fine.

| | |
|---|---|
| 1/2 cup | fresh strawberries |
| 1/4 cup | low-fat or non-fat yogurt |
| 1 clove | garlic, chopped |
| 1/4 cup | olive oil |
| 2 tbsp | vinegar |
| 1 tbsp | lemon juice |
| 1 tsp | sugar or sweetener equivalent |
| 1 tsp | dried thyme |
| | Lettuce leaves |
| 1/2 cup | croutons (optional) |
| | Black pepper |
| | Sliced strawberries |

SUGGESTED SIDE DISHES:
- Salsa with corn chips
- Bread with tomatoes and Parmesan

VARIATIONS:
- Replace strawberries with other berries.
- Use some of the salad dressing as a marinade for grilled chicken or fish.

LOW-FAT OPTION:
- Instead of oil, use apple juice or strawberry-cranberry juice.

In a blender or with a hand blender, purée strawberries, yogurt, garlic, oil, vinegar, lemon juice, sugar and thyme till thick but not liquid. Drizzle the dressing over the lettuce and toss well. Garnish with croutons (if using), freshly ground pepper and strawberries.

**PREPARATION TIME:** *10–15 minutes*

# SLICED TOMATOES AND BASIL WITH TWO CHEESES

*Serves 4–6.*

| | |
|---|---|
| 2 tbsp | olive oil |
| 1 tbsp | wine or flavored vinegar |
| 1 clove | garlic, chopped |
| 2 | large ripe tomatoes |
| 6 | large basil leaves, chopped (or 1 tsp dried) |
| 1/3 cup | shredded mozzarella cheese |
| 1/4 cup | grated Parmesan cheese |
| 1/2 tsp | black pepper |

SUGGESTED SIDE DISHES:
- Salsa with corn chips
- Bread with tomatoes and Parmesan

In a bowl, whisk together the oil, vinegar and garlic. Slice the tomatoes (not too thin) and arrange on a serving plate. Sprinkle basil on the tomatoes. Drizzle the dressing over the tomatoes. Sprinkle the mozzarella on the tomatoes and sprinkle the Parmesan on top. Sprinkle with the black pepper and serve immediately.

**PREPARATION TIME:** *10–15 minutes*

VARIATIONS:
- Add grilled chicken or fish to make a complete meal.
- Replace mozzarella with sliced bocconcini.

LOW-FAT OPTION:
- Use low-fat yogurt or low-fat sour cream instead of oil.

# No-Mayo, No-Oil Caesar Salad

*Serves 4–6.*

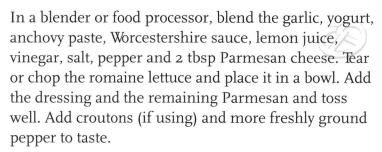

| | |
|---|---|
| 4 cloves | garlic |
| 1/4 cup | low-fat yogurt |
| 1 tsp | anchovy paste OR 1 anchovy, mashed |
| 1 tbsp | Worcestershire sauce |
| 1 tsp | lemon juice |
| 1 tsp | balsamic vinegar |
| 1/2 tsp | salt |
| 1/2 tsp | black pepper |
| 1/4 cup | grated Parmesan cheese |
| 1 large head | romaine lettuce |
| 1 cup | croutons (optional) |

SUGGESTED SIDE DISH:

• Bruschetta (recipe on p. 2)

In a blender or food processor, blend the garlic, yogurt, anchovy paste, Worcestershire sauce, lemon juice, vinegar, salt, pepper and 2 tbsp Parmesan cheese. Tear or chop the romaine lettuce and place it in a bowl. Add the dressing and the remaining Parmesan and toss well. Add croutons (if using) and more freshly ground pepper to taste.

**PREPARATION TIME:**     *10–15 minutes*

VARIATION:

— Use some of the salad dressing as a marinade for grilled chicken or fish.

# PEROGIES, PASTA AND GRAINS

I really liked your show on perogies. I learned a lot of things that I'm doing wrong when making perogies, things that were not mentioned in any of my cookbooks. Tell Helen thank you, I think she's great and I hope you have her feature on more of your shows.

Could you kindly send me Helen's recipe for perogies and cabbage rolls and any other recipes by Helen. I would also like copies of recipes for the shrimp, chicken and Italian casseroles...

Yours truly,

*L. T.*
Toronto, Ont.

# HELEN'S PEROGIES
*Serves 4–6.*

The "Helen's Perogies Show" was requested by our viewers, who sent letters wanting a perogie recipe. Having my mother on the show truly was a lot of fun *and* I made perogies for the first time in my life. Coming soon: "Helen's Cabbage Rolls."

**FILLING:**

| | |
|---|---|
| 2-1/2 lb | red potatoes, halved |
| 1 cup | milk |
| 2 tbsp | butter |
| 2 | onions, chopped |
| 1/2 lb | bacon, chopped |
| 6 oz | mild cheddar cheese |

**PEROGIE DOUGH:**

| | |
|---|---|
| 2 cups | all-purpose flour (approx.) |
| 1/2 tsp | salt |
| 1 cup | warm water |
| 1/4 cup | corn oil |

SUGGESTED SIDE DISHES:
- Borscht
- Kielbasa

**FILLING:**

Boil the potatoes until well done, drain, and mash with the milk and butter. Set aside. In a large skillet over medium heat, cook the onions and bacon together; be careful not to burn them. Reserve 1/2 cup of mixture for spooning over the cooked perogies. Add the remaining bacon and onions to the potatoes. Stir the cheese into the potato mixture. Mix well. Chill until very cold.

**PEROGIE DOUGH:**

Mix flour and salt in large bowl. Make a well in the middle; pour water and oil into the well. Mix together. Add more flour, 1/2 cup at a time until dough is firm. Knead dough until mixture does not stick to hands. Cover tightly and let stand for half an hour in a warm place.

# HELEN'S PEROGIES
*continued*

**PEROGIES:**

On a lightly floured surface, roll out dough to 1/4 inch thickness and cut in 2-inch-diameter circles. Add 1 tsp filling, fold over one half of circle and press the edges together to seal. Bring a large pot of water to the boil; add 1 tbsp of oil, and add perogies. Stir occasionally so perogies won't stick to the bottom. When the perogies rise to the top, add 1 cup of cold water to stop the cooking. Remove the perogies with a slotted spoon. Perogies will cook in 3–4 minutes. Serve topped with reserved onion-bacon mixture.

**PREPARATION TIME:**     *more than 30 minutes*

**TIME SAVER:**

Have Helen make them and ship them via AIR FROZEN. Make the dough the day before.

VARIATION:
— Mary Jo and my mother were going to replace *me*!

LOW-FAT OPTION:
— I don't think so!

# TRI-COLORED PASTA WITH PESTO
*Serves 4–6.*

I also brush this pesto sauce on chicken breasts and then broil them.

| | |
|---|---|
| 2 cups | tri-colored pasta |
| 2 cups | fresh basil |
| 2 tbsp | pine nuts |
| 4 cloves | garlic, chopped |
| 1/2 tsp | black pepper |
| 1/2 cup | olive oil |
| 1/4 cup | grated Parmesan cheese |

SUGGESTED SIDE DISHES:
- Marinated mushrooms
- Garlic bread
- Roasted peppers

Cook pasta in a large pot of boiling water until tender but firm. Drain and return to pot. In a food processor, process basil, pine nuts, garlic and pepper until smooth. With the motor running, slowly add olive oil and Parmesan. Pour pesto over tri-colored pasta and toss to coat well.

**PREPARATION TIME:**    *20–25 minutes*

**TIME SAVER:**
Use pre-cooked pasta.

TIP:
For a tasty appetizer, spread leftover pesto on sliced French bread and broil.

VARIATION:
Add cooked ground beef, chicken or turkey.

# SPAGHETTI WITH TOMATO SAUCE

*Serves 4–6.*

This dish is one of my favorites because it's so easy—and it proves that making pasta sauces from scratch doesn't have to be a lengthy process.

| | |
|---|---|
| 1 can | stewed tomatoes (19 oz/540 mL) |
| 2 tbsp | tomato paste |
| 1 tbsp | olive oil |
| 3 cloves | garlic, chopped |
| 1 tsp | lemon juice |
| 1 | small onion (or 2 shallots), chopped |
| 1/4 cup | chopped fresh dill |
| 1/2 tsp | salt |
| 1/2 tsp | pepper |
| 1/2 tsp | chopped hot pepper (optional) |
| 1/2 cup | chopped celery |
| 1 tsp | dried basil |
| 1 | bay leaf |
| 1 tsp | sugar or sweetener equivalent |
| 2 handfuls | spaghetti or other pasta |

**SUGGESTED SIDE DISHES:**
- Italian antipasto platter
- Marinated mushrooms
- Garlic bread
- Roasted peppers

In a food processor, chop fine the tomatoes, tomato paste, oil, garlic, lemon juice, onion, dill, salt, pepper and hot pepper (if using). Transfer to a large heavy saucepan. Add the celery, basil, bay leaf and sugar. Bring sauce to a boil; reduce heat and simmer, uncovered and stirring occasionally, 15–20 minutes. If liquid evaporates, just add some more water or tomato juice. Meanwhile, in a large pot of boiling water, cook spaghetti until tender but firm. Discard the bay leaf and spoon sauce over drained pasta.

**PREPARATION TIME:**    *20–25 minutes*

**TIME SAVER:**
Use pre-cooked pasta.

VARIATION:
Add ground beef, chicken or turkey cooked 5 minutes before serving and mix well into mixture.

LOW-FAT OPTION:
Leave out the oil.

# LOW-FAT TOMATO SAUCE
*Serves 6–8.*

This low-fat tomato sauce can be frozen and used later with pasta
or rice or as a base for some meat dishes. On air, we served this on
pork chops with Swiss cheese, as well as with spaghetti. We also
used this tomato sauce in the "Seafood Lasagna Show."

| | |
|---|---|
| 1 | medium onion, quartered |
| 3 cloves | garlic, chopped |
| 1/2 cup | whole mushrooms |
| 1/2 cup | sweet green or yellow pepper, diced |
| 1/2 cup | sweet red pepper, diced |
| 1/2 cup | diced carrots |
| 1/2 cup | fresh basil (or 2 tbsp dried) |
| 1/4 cup | chopped fresh oregano (or 1 tsp dried) |
| 1 cup | apple juice |
| 2 tbsp | tomato paste |
| 2 cans | tomatoes (each 28 oz/796 mL) |
| 1 tsp | salt |
| 1 tsp | black pepper |
| 1 | bay leaf |

**SUGGESTED SIDE DISH:**
• Asparagus

In a food processor, chop the onion, garlic,
mushrooms, peppers, carrots, basil and oregano.
Add apple juice, tomato paste, tomatoes, salt and
pepper; process to mix. Transfer to a large heavy
saucepan. Add bay leaf. Simmer, uncovered,
15–20 minutes or until desired thickness.
Discard bay leaf. Serve with pasta, rice, meat
dishes or seafood.

**PREPARATION TIME:**     *30 minutes*

**TIME SAVER:**
Use fresh pasta, which requires only 2–3
minutes of cooking time.

**TIPS:**
➤ Basil comes from the mint
family and is used to flavor
sauces, tomatoes, fish, poultry
and salads.
➤ Garlic is believed to be effective
in lowering cholesterol and
improving circulation.
➤ Pasta, with the exception of egg
noodles, is fat free, high in
complex carbohydrates and low
in calories.

**VARIATION:**
➤ If you want to add meat, use
ground turkey. Microwave it
first, drain off the excess fat and
add to the simmering sauce.

# PASTA WITH BLUE CHEESE AND SPINACH

*Serves 2–4.*

Pasta dishes can be as interesting as the ingredients you use. When throwing a dinner party, I often serve my guests a small portion of pasta as an appetizer.

| | |
|---|---|
| 1 | small onion, chopped |
| 2 cloves | garlic, minced |
| 2 cups | chopped spinach |
| 1/4 cup | chopped parsley |
| 1 tbsp | olive oil |
| 1 tsp | chopped fresh rosemary |
| 1/2 tsp | dried oregano |
| 1/2 tsp | salt |
| 1/2 tsp | black pepper |
| 1/4 cup | dry white wine |
| 2 cups | dry penne or bow-tie pasta |
| 1/2 cup | crumbled blue cheese |

SUGGESTED SIDE DISH:
• Grilled mushrooms

In a large skillet, sauté the onion, garlic, spinach and parsley in oil. Add the rosemary, oregano, salt, pepper and white wine. Simmer for 2–3 minutes or till the wine has reduced a bit. Meanwhile, cook pasta in a large pot of boiling water until tender but firm. Drain and return to pot. Stir the blue cheese into the sauce and gently heat through. Toss with pasta and serve immediately.

**PREPARATION TIME:**      *20 minutes*

**TIME SAVER:**
Use fresh pasta, or cook pasta in advance.

VARIATIONS:
— Replace blue cheese with a well-aged cheddar.
— Replace the onion with 4 shallots.
— Replace the white wine with red wine.

LOW-FAT OPTIONS:
— Replace the cheese with tofu.
— Replace the wine with grape juice.

# PASTA WITH OLIVES, MUSHROOMS AND FETA

*Serves 2–4.*

I first tasted a variation of this dish in Italy. I try different ingredients sometimes just for a change. The combination of olives and feta adds a really tangy flavor to this dish. This truly is one of my favorites.

| | |
|---|---|
| 1 | medium onion, chopped |
| 2 cloves | garlic, minced |
| 2 tbsp | olive oil |
| 1 cup | chopped mushrooms |
| 3/4 cup | crumbled feta cheese |
| 1/2 cup | chopped pitted olives |
| 1/2 cup | diced sweet red pepper |
| 1 tbsp | dried rosemary |
| 1 tsp | dried oregano |
| 1/2 cup | white wine |
| 1/2 pkg | pasta (450 g) |

SUGGESTED SIDE DISH:
• Grilled mushrooms

In a large skillet, sauté the onion and garlic in oil until translucent. Add the mushrooms, feta, olives and peppers; sauté another 3 minutes. Add the rosemary, oregano and white wine and reduce by half. Meanwhile, cook pasta in a large pot of boiling water until tender but firm. Drain and toss with sauce. Serve immediately.

**PREPARATION TIME:**     *20 minutes*

**TIME SAVER:**
Use fresh pasta, or cook pasta in advance.

VARIATIONS:
— Replace the onion with 6 shallots.
— Replace the white wine with red wine.

LOW-FAT OPTIONS:
— Replace the feta with tofu.
— Replace the wine with grape juice.

# Squeeze Me Mama's Smoked Salmon Pasta in Cream Sauce

*Serves 4.*

I first had this truly magnificent smoked salmon pasta dish in Rome. I begged "Mama"—the owner of the tiny restaurant—to allow me into the kitchen to watch her make another order. (Of course I had to eat the other order myself—but that wasn't a problem!)

| | |
|---|---|
| 2 tbsp | butter |
| 1 | small onion (or 4 shallots), chopped |
| 1/2 cup | finely chopped sweet red pepper |
| 2 cloves | garlic, minced |
| 3/4 cup | chopped smoked salmon |
| 1/2 cup | whipping cream |
| 1/2 cup | milk |
| 1 tbsp | fresh thyme (or 1/2 tsp dried) |
| 1/2 tsp | salt |
| 1/2 tsp | black pepper |
| 1/4 cup | grated Parmesan cheese |
| 2 cups | bow-tie pasta |

SUGGESTED SIDE DISHES:
- Bruschetta (recipe on p. 2)
- Endive salad

In a saucepan, melt the butter over medium heat. Sauté the onions and red pepper for one minute. Add the garlic and sauté another minute. Add the smoked salmon and sauté 2 minutes. Raise heat to medium and add the cream, milk, thyme, salt, half the black pepper and half the Parmesan cheese. Immediately reduce heat to low. Stir gently until the mixture starts to thicken, about 5 minutes. Do not allow mixture to boil or cream will curdle. Remove from heat and keep warm. In a large pot of boiling salted water, cook pasta until tender but firm. Drain. Pour sauce over pasta and toss gently. Sprinkle each serving with remaining Parmesan cheese.

**PREPARATION TIME:**     *20 minutes*

TIP:

Excellent as a vegetarian meal, too: replace the smoked salmon with 2 cups of chopped mushrooms and use soya milk instead of cream or milk.

LOW-FAT OPTIONS:

Replace whipping cream with 3/4 cup of low-fat or non-fat sour cream and replace milk with 1/2 cup of fat-free or low-fat milk.

Replace butter with calorie-reduced margarine.

# IBIZA SHRIMP-CLAM PASTA

*Serves 2–4.*

This impressive Mediterranean dish can be prepared in hardly any time at all. I first had a variation on this wonderful pasta dish in Ibiza, one of the Balearic Islands off the east coast of Spain.

| | |
|---|---|
| 2 cups | tri-colored pasta |
| 3 tbsp | olive oil |
| 1 | small onion (or 4 shallots), chopped |
| 2 cloves | garlic, minced |
| 1 cup | large shrimp, peeled and deveined |
| 1 can | clams, rinsed (14 oz) |
| 1/2 cup | chopped parsley |
| 1/2 tsp | salt |
| 1/2 tsp | black pepper |
| 1/4 cup | grated Parmesan cheese |

To a large pot of boiling salted water, add 1 tsp oil. Cook pasta until tender but firm. Meanwhile, in a large sauté pan, heat the 3 tbsp olive oil. Sauté the onions and garlic for 2 minutes. Do not burn the garlic. Add the shrimp and cook for 1 minute. Add the clams, parsley, salt and pepper. Cook another 5 minutes. Add drained pasta and Parmesan cheese to sauté pan and stir well. Serve immediately.

**PREPARATION TIME:**     *15 minutes*

**TIME SAVER:**

Cook your pasta in advance and then just mix into the sauté pan with the other ingredients at the end.

SUGGESTED SIDE DISHES:
- Tomatoes stuffed with herbs
- Steamed vegetables

TIPS:
- Fresh clams are available in the shell or shucked. Shucked clams should be plump and smell fresh.
- Buy shrimp with the shell on, as the shell helps protect the meat.
- Fresh pasta can be refrigerated for about a week or kept 2–3 months in the freezer.

VARIATIONS:
- To make this dish vegetarian, replace the clams and shrimp with chopped mushrooms, chopped sweet red peppers and some shredded carrot. (I've done it and love it.) About 5 minutes less.
- Replace the parsley with 1/4 cup fresh coriander.

LOW-FAT OPTION:
- Replace the olive oil with vegetable stock.

# SPAGHETTI WITH BLACK TIGER SHRIMP, GARLIC AND OLIVE OIL

*Serves 4–6.*

This pasta recipe is from the Mediterranean, where jumbo shrimp are plentiful.

| | |
|---|---|
| 3 cloves | garlic, chopped |
| 3 tbsp | olive oil |
| 2 | large sweet red peppers, sliced in strips |
| 8 | large tiger shrimp OR 12 jumbo shrimp, peeled and deveined |
| 1/2 cup | chopped flat-leaf parsley |
| 1/4 cup | apple juice |
| 1/2 tsp | hot sauce |
| 1 tbsp | lemon juice |
| 4 | green onions, sliced on the diagonal |
| 1 tsp | paprika |
| 1/2 tsp | salt |
| 1/2 tsp | black pepper |
| 2 handfuls | spaghetti |
| 1/4 cup | grated Parmesan cheese |

SUGGESTED SIDE DISHES:
- Bruschetta with zucchini
- Spinach salad
- Sliced Tomatoes and Basil with Two Cheeses (recipe on p. 19)

In a large skillet, sauté the garlic in 2 tbsp of the oil for 1 minute. Add the red pepper and the shrimp. Sauté, turning constantly, until the shrimp turn white. Add the remaining olive oil, half the parsley, apple juice, hot sauce, lemon juice, green onions, paprika, salt and pepper. Allow some of the liquid to cook away. Meanwhile, in a large pot of boiling water, cook spaghetti until tender but firm; drain and place on plates. Spoon the sauce onto the pasta and arrange the shrimp in a circle on top. Sprinkle with the remaining parsley and the Parmesan cheese.

**PREPARATION TIME:**     *20–25 minutes*

VARIATIONS:
- Replace shrimp with 1 can of clams.
- Replace fresh parsley with same amount of coriander; this will give a sharper taste.

# LOBSTER PENNE

*Serves 2.*

This lobster pasta was part of our "Valentine Special," an episode made more memorable by Mary Jo's "big" hair.

| | |
|---|---|
| 2 | lobster tails |
| 2 tbsp | butter |
| 2 cups | penne |
| 2 | small shallots, chopped |
| 2 cloves | garlic, minced |
| 1/4 cup | chopped fennel |
| 1/2 cup | dry white wine |
| 1 tbsp | dried tarragon |
| 1/2 tsp | paprika |
| 1/2 tsp | dried mint |
| 1/2 tsp | salt |
| 1/2 tsp | black pepper |
| 1 | bay leaf |
| 1/2 cup | table or half-and-half cream |
| 1/2 cup | sour cream |

SUGGESTED SIDE DISHES:
- Fruity Strawberry Salad (recipe on p. 18)
- Baked stuffed tomatoes
- Cream of Tomato Soup with Non-Fat Yogurt (recipe on p. 13)

Slice lobster tails 1 inch thick. In a medium skillet, gently cook lobster in 1 tbsp of the butter for 3–4 minutes till flesh turns white. Remove and set aside. In a large pot of boiling water, cook penne until tender but firm. Meanwhile, in the same skillet, melt remaining butter and sauté shallots, garlic and fennel until translucent. Add wine and bring to a boil. Add lobster, tarragon, paprika, mint, salt, pepper, bay leaf, table cream and sour cream. Reduce heat and simmer 6–8 minutes until heated through. Discard bay leaf. Serve sauce over drained penne or mix the cooked pasta into the sauce.

**PREPARATION TIME:**     *25–30 minutes*

VARIATION:
Replace the lobster with crab, crayfish or even monkfish.

LOW-FAT OPTION:
Use non-fat yogurt instead of cream and a low-fat sour cream.

# SEAFOOD LASAGNA
*Serves 6–8.*

This lasagna is a very light meal, and it uses a tomato sauce instead of a cream-based sauce. When my neighbor did this recipe, she added some smoked salmon—it was delicious. Experiment and have fun.

| | |
|---|---|
| 10–12 | lasagna noodles |
| 1 can | crushed tomatoes (28 oz/796 mL) |
| 2 cloves | garlic, minced |
| 1 | medium onion, chopped |
| 1 tsp | dried oregano (or 1/2 cup chopped fresh) |
| 1/2 tsp | salt |
| 1 tsp | black pepper |
| 1 cup | shrimp, peeled and deveined |
| 1 cup | crab meat |
| 1 cup | canned clams, rinsed |
| 1 cup | ricotta cheese |
| 1 | sweet red pepper, diced |
| 1 cup | shredded mozzarella cheese |
| 1/2 cup | grated Parmesan cheese |

SUGGESTED SIDE DISHES:
- No-Mayo, No-Oil Caesar Salad (recipe on p. 20)
- Bruschetta (recipe on p. 2)

*continued...*

# SEAFOOD LASAGNA
*continued*

If you are using dry lasagna noodles, boil 8–10 minutes; fresh, 2–3 minutes. (There is no need to pre-cook "instant" noodles.) Place cooked noodles in a bowl of lukewarm water to prevent sticking. Before placing in the baking dish, dry with paper towels. In a bowl, mix together the tomatoes, garlic, onion, oregano, salt and pepper. Coat bottom of a 13- x 9-inch baking dish with some of the tomato mixture. Place a layer of noodles in the baking dish. Spread a layer of sauce over noodles. Top sauce with a layer of assorted seafood, ricotta cheese, red peppers and some mozzarella and Parmesan cheese. Continue this layering process once more, finishing with remaining sauce, mozzarella and Parmesan. Ensure top layer of noodles is well coated with sauce to prevent the noodles from drying out. Bake uncovered at 375°F for 20–25 minutes or until cheese begins to brown.

**PREPARATION TIME:** *35 minutes*

**TIME SAVER:**
Use the pre-cooked or "instant" ready-for-the-oven lasagna noodles.

TIPS:
➤ When using canned clams, rinse them well to remove the excess salt.
➤ Shrimp are sold peeled and unpeeled. It's better to buy them with the shells on, as the shells protect the meat. Be sure the shells are firm and shiny and that they feel full.
➤ Partly skimmed ricotta cheese is a good source of calcium for strong teeth and bones. It's a better source than whole-milk ricotta.

VARIATIONS:
➤ Use tuna, smoked salmon, crab or mussels—or even ground chicken for non-seafood-lovers.
➤ Replace seafood with tofu for a vegetarian treat.
➤ Instead of oregano, use thyme. Lemon thyme is a good choice with seafood because of its citrus aroma and taste.

LOW-FAT OPTIONS:
➤ On the show we used our Low-Fat Tomato Sauce (recipe on p. 26).
➤ Use partly skimmed or low-fat cheddar or mozzarella.

# SPAGHETTI WITH GARLIC, OLIVES AND SAGE

*Serves 2–4.*

The "Vegetarian Pasta Show" was popular because it featured dishes that are not only delicious but also healthy and low in fat. I call the following three recipes "guilt free."

| | |
|---|---|
| 2 handfuls | spaghetti |
| 6 cloves | garlic, minced |
| 1 | medium onion, chopped |
| 2 tbsp | olive oil |
| 1/2 cup | pitted black olives, sliced |
| 2 tbsp | chopped fresh sage |
| 1/2 cup | dry white wine |
| 1/2 tsp | salt |
| 1/2 tsp | black pepper |
| 1/4 cup | grated Parmesan cheese |

SUGGESTED SIDE DISH:
- Bruschetta (recipe on p. 2)
- Chopped grilled vegetables

In a large pot of boiling water, cook spaghetti until tender but firm. Meanwhile, in a medium skillet, sauté garlic and onion in oil for 2–3 minutes. Add the olives and sage; sauté another 2–3 minutes. Add the wine, salt and pepper; simmer 2–3 minutes. Serve over drained spaghetti and sprinkle with Parmesan.

**PREPARATION TIME:**     *15–20 minutes*

**TIME SAVER:**
Allow your food processor to do all of the chopping.

VARIATION:
Add tofu.

LOW-FAT OPTION:
Use vegetable stock or juice instead of the oil.

# Penne with Peppers in Tomato-Basil Sauce
### Serves 2–4.

This recipe is a good vegetarian pasta dish. The sweet peppers and fresh basil add a delicate tangy flavor to the pasta.

| | |
|---|---|
| 2 | sweet red peppers, chopped |
| 1 | sweet green pepper, chopped |
| 1 | small onion, chopped |
| 1 tbsp | olive oil |
| 1/4 cup | red wine |
| 1/4 cup | frozen apple juice concentrate |
| 1 can | stewed tomatoes (19 oz/540 mL) |
| 1/4 cup | chopped fresh basil |
| 1 | bay leaf |
| 1/2 tsp | salt |
| 1/2 tsp | black pepper |
| 2 cups | penne |

SUGGESTED SIDE DISH:
- Bruschetta with chopped grilled vegetables

In a large sauté pan, sauté peppers and onion in oil 2–3 minutes. Add wine, apple juice concentrate, tomatoes, basil, bay leaf, salt and pepper; simmer 10–15 minutes, adjusting the heat so the liquid does not reduce too much. Discard the bay leaf. Meanwhile, in a large pot of boiling water, cook penne until tender but firm. Toss drained pasta with sauce and serve immediately.

**PREPARATION TIME:**       *15–20 minutes*

**TIME SAVER:**
Allow your food processor to do all of the chopping.

VARIATION:
— Add tofu.

LOW-FAT OPTION:
— Use vegetable stock or juice to replace the oil.

# RICE NOODLES WITH MUSHROOM SAUCE

*Serves 2–4.*

| | |
|---|---|
| 2 cups | chopped mushrooms |
| 2 cloves | garlic, minced |
| 1 | medium onion, chopped |
| 1/2 tsp | minced fresh ginger |
| 2 tbsp | vegetable or olive oil |
| 1 tsp | dried basil |
| 1 tsp | dried oregano |
| 1/2 tsp | salt |
| 1/2 tsp | black pepper |
| 1 cup | soya milk |
| 2 cups | rice noodles |

**SUGGESTED SIDE DISH:**
- Bruschetta with chopped grilled vegetables

In a large skillet, sauté mushrooms, garlic, onion and ginger in oil until translucent. Add basil, oregano, salt, pepper and soya milk; allow mixture to reduce by half. Meanwhile, in a large pot of boiling water, cook rice noodles until tender, about 3 minutes. Arrange drained noodles on plates and spoon sauce over.

**PREPARATION TIME:** *15–20 minutes*

**TIME SAVER:**
Allow your food processor to do all of the chopping.

**VARIATIONS:**
- Replace soya milk with 1/2 cup of cream.
- Replace the rice noodles with angel hair or capelli pasta.

**LOW-FAT OPTION:**
- Use vegetable stock or juice instead of the oil.

# MACARONI WITH TOFU, MUSHROOMS AND SPINACH
*Serves 4–6.*

The "Macaroni Show" was one of my favorites, as it reminded me of meals when I was growing up. My mother was truly a creative woman when it came to variations on macaroni and cheese.

| | |
|---|---|
| 1 can | tomatoes, drained (28 oz/796 mL) |
| 1/2 cup | fresh dill |
| 1/2 cup | fresh parsley |
| 2 cloves | garlic, chopped |
| 1 tbsp | tomato paste |
| 1/2 tsp | salt |
| 1/2 tsp | black pepper |
| 1/2 tsp | chili powder |
| 3 cups | macaroni |
| 1 tsp | olive oil |
| 1 cup | chopped mushrooms |
| 1 | small onion, diced |
| 2 cups | shredded fresh or frozen spinach |
| 1 lb | firm tofu, sliced |

SUGGESTED SIDE DISHES:
- Fresh broccoli salad with rice vinegar
- Lima bean salad with tomato salsa

In a food processor, blend tomatoes, dill, parsley, garlic, tomato paste, salt, pepper and chili powder. Set aside. In a large pot of boiling water, cook pasta until tender but firm. Meanwhile, in a large skillet, heat the oil and sauté mushrooms and onion until translucent. Gradually add spinach and tofu; cook until the corners of the tofu are golden. Do not overcook. Drain the pasta and return it to the pot. Add the tomato mixture and the tofu mixture and stir over low heat 1–2 minutes or until heated through.

**PREPARATION TIME:**     *20 minutes*

# Macaroni and Cheese Primavera

*Serves 4–6.*

| | |
|---|---|
| 3 cups | macaroni |
| 1/2 cup | sweet red pepper, diced |
| 1 | small onion, diced |
| 1 | small zucchini, diced |
| 1 tbsp | oil |
| 1 cup | shredded cheddar cheese |
| 1/2 cup | non-fat yogurt |
| 1/2 cup | milk |
| 2 | tomatoes, chopped |
| 1/2 tsp | salt |
| 1/2 tsp | black pepper |
| 1/4 cup | grated Parmesan cheese |

SUGGESTED SIDE DISHES:
- Green bean salad with garlic
- Cauliflower salad

In a large pot of boiling water, cook macaroni until tender but firm. Meanwhile, in a large skillet, sauté the red pepper, onion and zucchini in the oil 2–3 minutes. Drain pasta and return to pot. Add cooked vegetables, cheddar, yogurt, milk, tomatoes, salt and pepper. Mix well. Transfer to a nonstick 11- x 9-inch baking dish. Sprinkle with Parmesan cheese and bake, uncovered, at 350°F for 10–15 minutes. Cover if the top begins to burn.

**PREPARATION TIME:**     *20–25 minutes*

VARIATIONS:
- Add cooked ground meat or seafood to the primavera sauce.
- Replace zucchini with asparagus.

LOW-FAT OPTION:
- Use low-fat cheddar cheese.

# SPICY SEAFOOD PAELLA

*Serves 6–8.*

This is a truly quick version of the wonderfully flavorful Spanish rice dish, which starts on top of the stove and finishes in the oven. Mary Jo had a hard time pronouncing paella (PIE-ay-ya) when we prepared it on television.

| | |
|---|---|
| 2 tbsp | oil |
| 2 | medium onions, chopped |
| 1/2 cup | chopped celery |
| 3 cloves | garlic, minced |
| 1 | sweet red pepper, chopped |
| 1 | sweet green pepper, chopped |
| 3 | medium tomatoes, chopped |
| 2 cups | rice |
| 1/2 tsp | salt |
| 1-1/2 tsp | black pepper |
| 1/2 cup | chopped parsley |
| 1 | bay leaf |
| 1/4 tsp | saffron |
| 4 cups | boiling water |
| 1 cup | jumbo shrimp, peeled and deveined |
| 1 cup | medium scallops |
| 1 cup | clams, canned |
| 2 lb | fresh mussels |
| 1/2 tsp | chopped jalapeño pepper (optional) |

SUGGESTED SIDE DISHES:
- Green salad with raspberry vinaigrette
- Toasted bread with dill and garlic

# SPICY SEAFOOD PAELLA
*continued*

In a large oven-proof pot, heat the oil. Sauté the onions for 2 minutes. Add celery, garlic and red and green peppers; sauté for 2 minutes. Add the tomatoes, rice, salt, pepper, parsley, bay leaf, saffron and boiling water. Cover and simmer for 10 minutes. Arrange seafood on top of mixture and bake, covered, at 425°F for another 15–20 minutes or until rice is cooked and mussels open. Discard the bay leaf and any mussels that do not open.

**PREPARATION TIME:**     *30–45 minutes*

**TIME SAVERS:**
Cook the rice while you're chopping vegetables. Use canned chopped tomatoes rather than fresh. Use your food processor to chop the vegetables.

TIP:
Use a very heavy-bottomed pan.

VARIATION:
Add cooked sausage, pork or chicken and any other type of seafood.

# CHINESE FRIED RICE
*Serves 4–6.*

This dinner is based on one from my mother's neighbors in Winnipeg. You can add other types of meat such as pork or beef, or substitute seafood.

| | |
|---|---|
| 2 tbsp | vegetable oil |
| 2 cloves | garlic, minced |
| 1 | boneless chicken breast, sliced |
| 2 | eggs, beaten |
| 1 cup | large shrimp, peeled and deveined |
| 1 cup | green peas |
| 1 cup | bean sprouts |
| 1/2 cup | chopped broccoli |
| 1/2 cup | chopped parsley |
| 4 | green onions, chopped |
| 2 cups | cooked rice |
| 1/4 cup | light soy sauce |
| 1/2 tsp | black pepper |

SUGGESTED SIDE DISHES:
- Oriental cabbage salad
- Miso soup

In a wok or large heavy skillet, heat the oil. Quickly stir-fry chicken and cook for a few minutes till just done. Push chicken to sides of wok. Scramble the eggs in the wok; push to sides. Add garlic, shrimp, peas, bean sprouts, broccoli, parsley, half the green onions and the rice; mix together with chicken and eggs and stir-fry 4–5 minutes; do not burn. Add the soy sauce and pepper and stir-fry for another 2–3 minutes. Garnish with the remaining green onions.

**PREPARATION TIME:** *25 minutes*

VARIATIONS:
- Throw in 1 cup snow peas, or any other vegetables you have on hand.
- Replace garlic with 1/2 tsp chopped fresh ginger.

LOW-FAT OPTIONS:
- Remove the skin and fat from the chicken.
- Instead of oil, use a vegetable oil (canola) or, for even lower fat, vegetable stock.

# MOROCCAN CHICKEN COUSCOUS
*Serves 4–6.*

This dish, which combines chicken, herbs, vegetables and fruit, is something I was determined to duplicate after having the real thing in North Africa. This was our last show of the season, so things got a little emotional.

| | |
|---|---|
| 2 tbsp | olive oil |
| 6 | chicken pieces, with skin |
| 2 cloves | garlic, minced |
| 1 | medium onion, chopped |
| 1 | small zucchini, chopped |
| 8 | cherry tomatoes |
| 2 | carrots, sliced |
| 1 cup | sliced fresh or unsweetened canned pears |
| 1/2 cup | seedless grapes |
| 1/4 cup | pitted black olives |
| 1/4 cup | dates |
| 1 tbsp | chopped fresh oregano |
| 1 tbsp | chopped fresh rosemary |
| 1 | bay leaf |
| 1/2 tsp | salt |
| 1/2 tsp | black pepper |
| 2 cups | couscous |
| 2 cups | Low-Fat Tomato Sauce (recipe on p. 26) |
| 2 cups | water |
| 2 cups | boiling chicken stock |

SUGGESTED SIDE DISHES:
- Lamb stew
- Tabbouleh salad
- Hummus with pita bread

*continued...*

# MOROCCAN CHICKEN COUSCOUS
*continued*

In a large heavy skillet, heat 1 tbsp olive oil and sauté chicken 10–12 minutes until golden brown. Transfer chicken to a 9- x 12-inch casserole dish. Heat remaining olive oil in skillet and sauté garlic and onion. Add to casserole; add zucchini, cherry tomatoes, carrots, pears, grapes, olives, dates, oregano, rosemary, bay leaf, salt, pepper, couscous, tomato sauce, water and boiling stock. Bake at 375°F for 20–25 minutes or until chicken is cooked. Discard bay leaf.

**PREPARATION TIME:**     *30–35 minutes*

**TIME SAVER:**
Microwave the chicken and the firmer vegetables. Microwave the soup stock.

VARIATIONS:
- Replace chicken with turkey or lamb.
- Replace the pears with apple.

LOW-FAT OPTION:
- Remove the skin and fat from the chicken.

# POULTRY

# POACHED CHICKEN IN RED WINE WITH FRESH HERBS

*Serves 4.*

I love this recipe because it tastes great and is so low in fat. I usually poach more chicken than I need and use it later sliced on a salad for lunch.

| | |
|---|---|
| 2 cups | water |
| 1/2 cup | red wine |
| 1 tsp | chopped fresh basil |
| 1 tsp | chopped fresh rosemary |
| 1 tsp | chopped fresh oregano |
| 1 clove | garlic, crushed |
| 2 | shallots, finely chopped |
| 1 | sweet red pepper, chopped |
| 1 tsp | balsamic vinegar |
| 1/4 tsp | salt |
| 1/2 tsp | black pepper |
| 1 | bay leaf |
| 4 | boneless skinless chicken breasts |

In a large deep skillet, bring to a boil the water, wine, basil, rosemary, oregano, garlic, shallots, red pepper, balsamic vinegar, salt, pepper and the bay leaf. Reduce heat and simmer for about 10 minutes, and then add the chicken. Poach the chicken until it is completely white and not pink inside, about 15–20 minutes.

**PREPARATION TIME:**     *25–30 minutes*

**TIME SAVER:**
Purchase chicken breasts already skinned and boned. This costs more but will save you some time and mess.

SUGGESTED SIDE DISHES:
- Assorted grilled vegetables
- Mixed leaf lettuce salad with lemon juice

TIP:
Discard the bay leaf and use the poaching liquid as a base for soups and sauces.

VARIATION:
Substitute seafood for chicken and poach for 20–25 minutes.

LOW-FAT OPTIONS:
For even lower calories, replace the red wine with unsweetened apple or grape juice.

Instead of chicken, prepare this dish with white fish.

If replacing chicken with turkey breast, poach a little longer to prevent toughness.

# POACHED RASPBERRY OR CRANBERRY CHICKEN

*Serves 2–4.*

This combination of chicken and fruit is very flavorful. Poaching is a low-calorie way of cooking.

| | |
|---|---|
| 4 | boneless chicken breasts or pieces |
| 1 tsp | oil |
| 1 | small onion (or 2 shallots), chopped |
| 1 cup | raspberry or cranberry juice |
| 1/4 cup | frozen raspberry or cranberry juice concentrate |
| 1/4 cup | red wine |
| 1/4 cup | chopped fresh tarragon |
| 1 tbsp | chopped fresh rosemary |
| 1/2 tsp | salt |
| 1 tsp | black pepper |
| 1 | bay leaf |
| 1 cup | fresh or frozen raspberries or cranberries |

**SUGGESTED SIDE DISHES:**
- Warm pear salad with spinach and bacon dressing
- Rice with spinach and basil

In a large skillet, sauté the chicken in oil on both sides 5–8 minutes or until brown. Remove and set aside. In the skillet, sauté the onion until translucent. Add juice, concentrate, red wine, tarragon, rosemary, salt, pepper and bay leaf. Simmer. Add chicken and poach, covered, for 12–15 minutes or until chicken is no longer pink inside. In the remaining 5 minutes, add the raspberries or cranberries. Serve on platter whole or sliced with poaching mixture and topped with berries.

**PREPARATION TIME:** *25–30 minutes*

**TIME SAVER:**
Microwave the chicken and add to the sauce when simmering.

**VARIATIONS:**
- Replace the chicken with lamb chops or steaks or with seafood.
- Replace the berries with any others in season.

**LOW-FAT OPTIONS:**
- Remove skin and fat from chicken.
- Replace red wine with fruit juice.

# CHICKEN TUSCANY

*Serves 4.*

This is a wonderful Italian recipe! If you want a different flavor, experiment with other herbs. In Tuscany, for instance, the main herb used in this dish is sage.

| | |
|---|---|
| 2 tbsp | olive oil |
| 2 | each chicken legs and breasts |
| 1 | red onion, chopped |
| 2 cloves | garlic, chopped |
| 1 cup | chopped mushrooms |
| 1 tbsp | chopped fresh rosemary |
| 1/2 tsp | dried basil |
| 1 | bay leaf |
| 2 | tomatoes, cut into chunks |
| 1 tsp | tomato paste |
| 3/4 cup | dry white wine |
| 1/2 tsp | salt |
| 1/2 tsp | black pepper |

**SUGGESTED SIDE DISHES:**

• Risotto
• Eggplant rolled up in a pita

In a large skillet, heat 1 tbsp of the olive oil and sauté chicken on each side till brown, about 4 minutes each side. Remove chicken and set aside. To the skillet, add the remaining oil and sauté the onion and garlic until translucent. Add the mushrooms and sauté another minute. Add the rosemary, basil, bay leaf, tomatoes, tomato paste, white wine, salt and pepper. Add chicken and simmer another 20–25 minutes or until chicken is no longer pink inside. Discard the bay leaf. When serving, spoon the sauce on top.

**PREPARATION TIME:**     *30–35 minutes*

**TIME SAVER:**

Pre-cook the chicken pieces in the microwave for 3–4 minutes. Use a food processor to chop the vegetables.

VARIATIONS:

— Replace the chicken with turkey pieces; you may have to simmer a few minutes longer.

— Replace the chicken with lean veal or stewing beef.

— Replace some of the herbs with others such as sage and thyme.

LOW-FAT OPTION:

— Remove the skin and fat from the chicken.

# CHICKEN AND SPINACH ROLL-UP

*Serves 4–6.*

This fast and easy roll-up is one of my favorite recipes; everyone who tries it loves it. At a dinner in Paris, I made this for friends—and they raved about it for days.

| | |
|---|---|
| 2 cloves | garlic, chopped |
| 1 cup | chopped spinach |
| 1/4 cup | Dijon mustard |
| 1/4 cup | yogurt |
| 1/2 tsp | salt |
| 1 tsp | black pepper |
| | Juice of 1 lemon |
| 4 | large boneless skinless chicken breasts |
| 6 slices | Swiss cheese |
| 4 thin slices | smoked turkey breast |
| 4 slices | lemon |

SUGGESTED SIDE DISHES:
- Steamed vegetables
- Crushed tomatoes and herbs
- Leaf lettuce with vinaigrette dressing

In a bowl, combine the garlic, spinach, mustard, yogurt, salt, half the pepper and 1 tsp lemon juice. Gently pound the chicken breasts flat between sheets of plastic wrap. Spread the sauce on the chicken. Top each breast with a slice of Swiss cheese and a slice of turkey. Cut remaining slices of cheese in half and set aside. Roll up the chicken and secure with a toothpick. Arrange in a nonstick baking dish and top each roll-up with half a slice of Swiss cheese and a slice of lemon. Bake at 375°F for 20–25 minutes or until chicken is no longer pink inside. Sprinkle with remaining pepper and lemon juice and serve immediately. (Slice the roll-ups prior to serving to get 6 portions.)

**PREPARATION TIME:** *30–35 minutes*

VARIATIONS:
- Replace the Swiss cheese with emmenthal or mozzarella.
- Replace spinach with finely chopped parsley.
- Replace smoked turkey breast with ham.

LOW-FAT OPTIONS:
- Use non-fat yogurt or low-fat sour cream.
- Replace Swiss cheese with skim-milk mozzarella.

# CHICKEN WITH DIJON MUSTARD AND CHEDDAR CHEESE

*Serves 4.*

This flavorful combination of mustard, cheddar and chicken will leave the impression you've spent twice the amount of time preparing it.

| | |
|---|---|
| 2 tbsp | olive oil |
| 2 tbsp | fresh thyme (or 1/2 tsp dried) |
| 1 | bay leaf |
| 4 | boneless chicken breasts |
| 1/4 cup | dry white wine |
| 1/2 cup | whipping cream |
| 2 tbsp | Dijon mustard |
| 1/4 tsp | salt |
| 1 cup | shredded cheddar cheese |
| 1/4 cup | grated Parmesan cheese |
| 1/4 cup | dry bread crumbs |
| 1/2 tsp | black pepper |

SUGGESTED SIDE DISHES:
- Carrots and bacon, or green beans and almonds
- Rice with spinach

In a large skillet, heat 1 tbsp of the olive oil with thyme and bay leaf. Gently brown the chicken, 6–8 minutes each side. Cover skillet, reduce the heat to medium and cook another 5 minutes or until the chicken is tender and no longer pink inside. Discard the bay leaf. Transfer the chicken to a nonstick baking dish. Drain fat from skillet. Add the remaining oil, white wine, cream, mustard, salt, half the cheddar and half the Parmesan. Stir for about 2 minutes or until the cheese has melted and the sauce is smooth; do not let the sauce boil. Pour sauce over chicken and sprinkle with remaining cheese, bread crumbs and pepper. Broil 3–5 minutes, until brown.

**PREPARATION TIME:**     *20–25 minutes*

VARIATIONS:
- Use gruyère cheese instead of cheddar.
- Replace chicken with turkey breast.

LOW-FAT OPTIONS:
- Replace white wine with grape juice.
- Replace whipping cream with low-fat sour cream or low-fat yogurt. (An 8 oz serving of yogurt contains 30–45% of your daily calcium requirement.)

# QUICK AND EASY COQ AU VIN

*Serves 4–6.*

This coq au vin will certainly impress friends, particularly when you tell them much of the fat content has been reduced.

| | |
|---|---|
| 2 cups | chicken stock |
| 2 cups | red wine |
| 1 tsp | dried dill |
| 1/2 tsp | dried oregano |
| 1/2 tsp | dried thyme |
| 1 | bay leaf |
| 1/2 tsp | salt |
| 1 tsp | black pepper |
| 5 lb | stewing chicken pieces |
| 1/2 lb | bacon, chopped |
| 2 | medium onions, chopped |
| 2 cloves | garlic, minced |
| 1/2 cup | chopped carrots |
| 1/2 cup | chopped celery |
| 1 tbsp | butter |
| 1 cup | sliced mushrooms |

SUGGESTED SIDE DISHES:
- Baked butternut squash
- Avocado salad with tomatoes and ricotta cheese
- Buttered dill noodles
- Egg noodles

In a crock pot or large sauce pan bring to a boil the stock, wine, dill, oregano, thyme, bay leaf, salt and pepper. Reduce to a simmer. Meanwhile, microwave chicken at High for approximately 5–7 minutes. Meanwhile, in a large nonstick skillet, sauté bacon until soft. Add the onions, garlic, carrots and celery and sauté until partially cooked. Remove and set aside. Melt butter in skillet and sauté chicken for 10 minutes. Add to the sauce with reserved vegetables; simmer another 10–15 minutes or until liquid is reduced and chicken is cooked. Add mushrooms and cook another 8–10 minutes. Discard the bay leaf.

VARIATIONS:
- Replace red with white wine.
- Substitute turkey or lean stewing beef for the chicken.

LOW-FAT OPTIONS:
- Leave out the bacon.
- Stew all the vegetables rather than sautéing them.

**PREPARATION TIME:** *30–40 minutes*

# ROASTED HERB CHICKEN WITH POTATOES AND CARROTS

*Serves 2–4.*

This is a great one-dish meal that allows you time with family and friends.

| | |
|---|---|
| 1 tbsp | olive oil |
| 2 | cloves garlic, minced |
| 1 | onion, chopped |
| 1 | chicken (3–4 lb), cut into serving pieces |
| 1 tsp | dried basil |
| 1 tsp | dried tarragon |
| 1 tsp | paprika |
| 1/2 cup | lemon juice |
| 1/2 tsp | salt |
| 1/2 tsp | black pepper |
| 2 sprigs | fresh rosemary |
| 4 | potatoes, chopped |
| 4 | carrots, chopped |
| 2 tbsp | chopped fresh mint |

SUGGESTED SIDE DISHES:
- Marinated potatoes and carrots
- Cream of broccoli soup
- Green salad with walnuts and Dijon vinaigrette

In a large skillet, heat the oil. Over low heat, cook the garlic, half the onion and the chicken until chicken is brown, about 10 minutes. Transfer the chicken to a baking dish and add the rest of the onion, basil, tarragon, paprika, lemon juice, salt, pepper and 1 sprig of rosemary. Arrange the potatoes and carrots around the sides and sprinkle with mint. Bake, uncovered, at 375°F about 25 minutes until chicken is no longer pink inside and vegetables are tender. Garnish with remaining sprig of rosemary.

**PREPARATION TIME:** *30–40 minutes*

**TIME SAVER:**
If you microwave the chicken while chopping the vegetables you will save 10 minutes in cooking time.

VARIATION:
— Replace the chicken with turkey.

LOW-FAT OPTIONS:
— Remove the skin and fat from the chicken.
— Microwave or poach the chicken, rather than sautéing it.

# BROILED CHICKEN WITH FENNEL AND TOMATO
*Serves 4.*

Broiled chicken with fennel is a wonderful combination and fairly low in fat. To make it more so, sauté the chicken in a nonstick pan in vegetable stock. (On this particular episode, Mary Jo poked fun at my skill with an appliance.)

| | |
|---|---|
| 1/2 cup | chopped fennel |
| 1/2 tsp | dried basil |
| 1/2 tsp | dried tarragon |
| 1/2 | sweet red pepper |
| 1/2 | sweet green pepper |
| 1/4 cup | frozen apple juice concentrate, thawed |
| 2 cloves | garlic, chopped |
| 2 | green onions |
| 1 can | tomatoes (14 oz/398 mL) |
| 1 tsp | paprika |
| 1/2 tsp | salt |
| 1/2 tsp | black pepper |
| 4 | skinless chicken breasts |
| 1 tbsp | olive oil |

SUGGESTED SIDE DISHES:
- Greek tomato salad with feta cheese
- Asparagus or zucchini grilled with lemon and mint
- Pasta with capers, olives and lemon

In a blender or food processor, add chopped fennel, basil, tarragon, red pepper, green pepper, apple juice concentrate, garlic, green onions and tomatoes. Process until chunky. Set aside. Sprinkle paprika, salt and pepper on both sides of chicken. In a large skillet, heat the oil and sauté chicken 8–10 minutes until browned. Transfer chicken to a baking dish and pour sauce over top. Bake, uncovered, at 350°F for 10–12 minutes, then broil for 2 minutes or until top is browned.

VARIATIONS:
- Replace chicken with turkey breast.
- Use fresh tomatoes, 1 cup of water and 1 tsp of tomato paste instead of canned tomatoes.
- Replace the fennel with celery.

**PREPARATION TIME:** *25–30 minutes*

**TIME SAVER:**
Pre-cook chicken in microwave and skip the sautéing.

# PACIFIC NORTHWEST CHICKEN WITH SWEET RED PEPPER SAUCE

*Serves 2–4.*

I first tried a version of this chicken dish in Seattle, Washington. I had to arm-wrestle the cook to divulge his secret recipe. With a few culinary twists of my own, I reveal to you this tasty, visually pleasing chicken delight. The red pepper sauce is also great with seafood.

| | |
|---|---|
| 1 | sweet red pepper |
| 4 | shallots or 1 small onion |
| 1/4 cup | apple juice |
| 1 tsp | sugar or sweetener equivalent |
| 1 tsp | hot sauce (optional) |
| 1/2 cup | chopped fresh parsley (or 1 tbsp dried) |
| 1 tsp | paprika |
| 1/2 tsp | salt |
| 1/2 tsp | black pepper |
| 1/4 cup | fresh thyme (or 1 tsp dried) |
| 4 | boneless skinless chicken breasts |

In a bowl with a hand blender or in a food processor, chop the red pepper and shallots. Add the apple juice, sugar, hot sauce (if using), and half the parsley. Blend well. Transfer sauce to a microwave-safe bowl and set aside. In a small bowl, combine the paprika, salt, pepper and thyme. Sprinkle over the chicken. Grill the chicken 10–15 minutes depending on thickness. (Make sure the chicken has grill marks.) Place on warm serving plate. Microwave the sweet pepper sauce, covered, at High for 2–3 minutes. Pour the sauce over the chicken and sprinkle with remaining parsley.

**PREPARATION TIME:**     *25–30 minutes*

SUGGESTED SIDE DISHES:
- White rice with red lima beans and spinach
- Pita bread with fresh vegetables and cheese

TIPS:
- Sweet red peppers are the caviar of vegetables and are higher in vitamin C than green peppers.
- When buying peppers, look for firm, shiny, bright-colored ones.
- Slightly wilted parsley can be revived in cold water.

VARIATIONS:
- Substitute turkey or tuna steaks for the chicken.
- Replace fresh thyme with dried or fresh oregano or tarragon.

# CHICKEN WITH VEGETABLES AND WINE

*Serves 2–4.*

The mixture of vegetables and herbs gives this dish a fresh, light flavor. Experiment with flavors by adding ginger for an Oriental twist or ground coriander and curry to make a wonderful Indian dish. As we always emphasize on "What's for Dinner?"—experiment.

| | |
|---|---|
| 4 | boneless chicken breasts |
| 2 tbsp | olive oil |
| 1 | small onion (or 2 shallots), chopped |
| 1 | small zucchini, julienned |
| 1 | sweet red pepper, julienned |
| 1 | sweet yellow pepper, julienned |
| 4 | large carrots, julienned |
| 1 cup | chopped broccoli |
| 1 cup | chopped squash |
| 1/2 cup | dry white wine |
| 1/4 cup | chopped fresh dill |
| 2 tbsp | chopped fresh basil |
| 1 tbsp | chopped fresh oregano |
| 2 | tomatoes, chopped |
| 1/2 tsp | salt |
| 1/2 tsp | black pepper |

SUGGESTED SIDE DISHES:
- Asparagus and leek soup
- Potato au gratin
- Waldorf salad

*continued...*

Flatten the chicken between sheets of plastic wrap and slice into strips 1/2 inch thick. Heat oil in a large heavy saucepan and sauté the chicken 2–4 minutes. Remove the chicken and set aside. Add the onion to the pan and sauté for 1 minute. Add the zucchini, red pepper, yellow pepper, carrots, broccoli and squash; sauté for 4 minutes. Reduce heat and add the wine, dill, basil, oregano, tomatoes, salt and pepper; simmer for 2 minutes. Return the chicken to the pan and simmer another 8–10 minutes until chicken is no longer pink inside. Serve topped with vegetables.

**PREPARATION TIME:** *25–30 minutes*

**TIME SAVER:**
Microwave some of the harder vegetables in advance. Use leftover chicken and allow it to simmer longer in the sauce.

VARIATIONS:
- Replace chicken with turkey or fish. If using fish, reduce the cooking time.
- Replace zucchini with more squash.
- For a vegetarian meal, replace chicken with sliced tofu.
- You can use red wine in place of white wine.

LOW-FAT OPTIONS:
- Remove skin and fat from chicken.
- Replace oil with chicken broth.
- Replace the white wine with grape juice.

# CHICKEN ROASTED WITH GARLIC

*Serves 2–4.*

The aroma and flavor created by the garlic and herbs will have everyone asking for this dish again and again. I first had a version of this recipe in California and remember eating about four or five cloves of garlic; I wasn't kissing anyone that evening!

| | |
|---|---|
| 3 | potatoes, cubed |
| 1 tbsp | olive oil |
| 1 | roasting chicken (3–4 lb), cut into serving pieces |
| 30 cloves | garlic, peeled |
| 1 | medium red onion, cut into large wedges |
| 2 | medium carrots, coarsely chopped |
| 2 tbsp | chopped fresh rosemary |
| 1 tsp | chopped fresh sage |
| 1/2 tsp | salt |
| 1/2 tsp | black pepper |
| 1/2 cup | chicken stock |
| 1 tsp | paprika |

**SUGGESTED SIDE DISHES:**
- Minestrone soup
- Vegetable salad with peanut-butter-and-honey dressing

Microwave the potatoes, covered, on High for 3 minutes. In a large heavy skillet, heat the oil. Sauté chicken 10–12 minutes until crispy and lightly browned. Transfer to casserole dish. Arrange garlic cloves, onion, carrots and potatoes around chicken. Sprinkle with the rosemary, sage, salt and pepper. Add the stock. Sprinkle with paprika. Roast, uncovered, at 400°F for 20–25 minutes or until chicken is no longer pink inside.

**PREPARATION TIME:**  *30–40 minutes*

**TIME SAVER:**

Microwave the meat, chicken stock and carrots to reduce cooking time by 8–10 minutes.
Use a food processor to chop the vegetables and herbs.

TIP:
Blanch the garlic in water and gently squeeze each clove to remove the skin.

VARIATIONS:
Replace chicken with turkey.
Replace the carrots with turnip or squash.

LOW-FAT OPTIONS:
Remove the skin and fat from the chicken.
Don't sauté the chicken. Add 1 cup more soup stock and stew the dish a bit longer.

# CHICKEN STUFFED WITH CRAB AND FRESH HERBS IN MUSTARD SAUCE

*Serves 4.*

This is one of my favorite meals. The combination of chicken and crab meat, with the tang of Dijon, is a must to try.

| | |
|---|---|
| 4 | boneless chicken breasts |
| 6 tbsp | Dijon mustard |
| 1 cup | fresh or canned crab meat |
| 1/2 cup | chopped spinach |
| 1/4 cup | chopped fresh parsley |
| 1/4 cup | chopped fresh basil |
| 1/4 cup | chopped fresh oregano |
| 3 tbsp | butter |
| 2 | shallots, chopped |
| 1/4 cup | dry white wine |
| 1/2 cup | non-fat yogurt |

SUGGESTED SIDE DISHES:
- Pineapple salsa
- Four-bean salad
- Lemon rice

Gently pound chicken flat between sheets of plastic wrap. Brush each breast with 2 tsp mustard. In a bowl, mix the crab meat, 2 tbsp of the mustard, spinach, parsley, basil and oregano. Spread the mixture onto the chicken breasts and roll them up, securing each with two toothpicks. In a large skillet, melt 2 tbsp of the butter and gently sauté the chicken, turning occasionally, 10–15 minutes depending on thickness of the meat, until cooked through. Remove and set aside. Melt remaining butter in the skillet and sauté the shallots, wine and the remaining mustard. Simmer 2–3 minutes. Add the yogurt and simmer another minute; do not boil. Return the chicken to the pan and simmer 2–3 minutes more until chicken is heated through. To serve, spoon sauce over the chicken.

# CHICKEN STUFFED WITH CRAB AND FRESH HERBS IN MUSTARD SAUCE

*continued*

**PREPARATION TIME:**     *25–35 minutes*

**TIME SAVER:**

Prepare the crab mixture in advance; keep covered and refrigerated.

Chop the parsley, spinach, basil and oregano in the food processor.

VARIATIONS:

- Replace crab with shrimp.
- Replace spinach with parsley.
- Replace the non-fat yogurt with low-fat sour cream; the sauce will be creamier.
- Replace seafood with cheese. Try using ricotta, Parmesan or goat cheese.

LOW-FAT OPTIONS:

- Replace the white wine with low-sodium soup stock.
- Use calorie-reduced butter or margarine.

# Tandoori Chicken

*Serves 4.*

Tandoori chicken is an Indian dish that you can serve either hot or cold.
The combination of spices and herbs not only gives the chicken a
wonderful flavor but also makes the dish very colorful.

| | |
|---|---|
| 1/4 cup | lemon juice |
| 1 cup | non-fat yogurt OR 1/2 cup low-fat sour cream |
| 3 cloves | garlic, crushed |
| 1 tbsp | paprika |
| 1 tsp | cumin |
| 1 tsp | turmeric |
| 1 tsp | ginger |
| 1/4 tsp | curry powder (optional) |
| 1/2 tsp | salt |
| 1/2 tsp | black pepper |
| 4 | chicken breasts |

**SUGGESTED SIDE DISHES:**

- Focaccia with fresh rosemary
- Mango salsa
- Basmati rice with apple juice and apples

In a bowl, stir together lemon juice, yogurt, garlic,
paprika, cumin, turmeric, ginger, curry powder
(if using), salt and pepper. Marinate chicken breasts,
covered, in yogurt sauce 10–15 minutes. Grill the
chicken, basting every 2–3 minutes with some of the
sauce, about 15 minutes or until chicken is tender and
no longer pink inside.

**VARIATION:**
— Replace chicken with swordfish or tuna.

**LOW-FAT OPTION:**
— Remove skin and fat from chicken.

**PREPARATION TIME:**     *25–30 minutes*

**TIME SAVER:**
Prepare marinade the night before; this will add flavor.

# SPICY SOUTHERN FRIED CHICKEN

*Serves 4.*

This is traditional southern American fare. Alter the spiciness of the fried chicken to your taste. When we made this dish on air, the cameramen fought over who was going to get more.

| | |
|---|---|
| 4 | eggs |
| 1/2 cup | all-purpose flour |
| 2 tsp | paprika |
| 1/2 tsp | sage |
| 1/4 tsp | cayenne pepper |
| 1/4 tsp | salt |
| 1/2 tsp | pepper |
| 3 cups | canola or safflower oil |
| 2 | fryer chickens, cut into serving pieces |

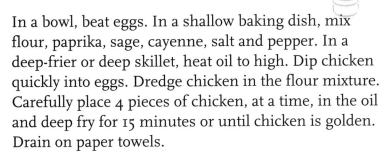

**SUGGESTED SIDE DISHES:**
- Garlic mashed potatoes with dill
- Peas and sautéed onions
- No-Mayo, No-Oil Caesar Salad (recipe on p. 20)

In a bowl, beat eggs. In a shallow baking dish, mix flour, paprika, sage, cayenne, salt and pepper. In a deep-frier or deep skillet, heat oil to high. Dip chicken quickly into eggs. Dredge chicken in the flour mixture. Carefully place 4 pieces of chicken, at a time, in the oil and deep fry for 15 minutes or until chicken is golden. Drain on paper towels.

**PREPARATION TIME:**     *30 minutes*

**TIME SAVER:**
Buy already cut up chicken.
Microwave chicken first for 3 minutes; do not overcook it.

VARIATION:
For less spicy chicken, replace the cayenne pepper with paprika or leave it out completely.

LOW-FAT OPTION:
Remove the skin and fat from the chicken.

# CHICKEN OR TURKEY MEATBALLS
*Serves 4–6.*

These meatballs are great with rice or pasta, and as an appetizer.

## SAUCE:

| | |
|---|---|
| 1 can | crushed or stewed tomatoes (19 oz/540 mL) |
| 1 | small onion, chopped |
| 2 cloves | garlic, minced |
| 1/2 tsp | dried basil |
| 1 tsp | tomato paste |
| 1/2 | sweet red pepper, diced |
| 1 | bay leaf |
| 1/2 tsp | salt |
| 1/2 tsp | black pepper |

## MEATBALLS:

| | |
|---|---|
| 2 lb | lean ground chicken or turkey |
| 1 | egg, lightly beaten |
| 1 | small tomato, chopped |
| 1 | small onion, chopped |
| 1/2 | sweet red pepper, chopped |
| 1 clove | garlic, minced |
| 1/2 cup | dry bread crumbs |
| 1/2 cup | chopped fresh dill |
| 1/2 tsp | chopped hot or jalapeño pepper |
| 1/2 tsp | salt |
| 1/2 tsp | black pepper |
| 1/4 cup | all-purpose flour |
| 2 tbsp | olive oil |

SUGGESTED SIDE DISHES:
- Sun-dried tomatoes and goat cheese in phyllo pastry
- Mediterranean salad with asiago cheese

## SAUCE:

In a heavy saucepan, stir together the tomatoes, onion, garlic, basil, tomato paste, red pepper, bay leaf, salt and pepper. Simmer 10–15 minutes, stirring occasionally.

# CHICKEN OR TURKEY MEATBALLS
*continued*

**MEATBALLS:**

Meanwhile, in a large bowl, mix together the ground meat, egg, tomato, onion, red pepper, garlic, bread crumbs, dill, hot pepper, salt and pepper. Shape into 12–15 small to medium-sized meatballs. Roll the balls in flour. In a large skillet, heat the oil and sauté the meatballs, turning occasionally, 12–15 minutes till they brown on all sides. Drain on paper towels.
Add the meatballs to the sauce and simmer another 2–3 minutes. Discard the bay leaf. Serve over rice, linguine or spaghetti, topped with grated Parmesan cheese and freshly ground black pepper.

**PREPARATION TIME:**     *25–30 minutes*

**TIME SAVER:**

Prepare the meatball mixture in advance and refrigerate, covered, until you're ready to cook dinner. Mix the meatball mixture in a food processor.

VARIATIONS:
➤ Substitute lean ground beef or ground lamb for the chicken or turkey.
➤ Replace the meat with one block of tofu; mix it in well and add 1/2 cup bread crumbs.
➤ Replace dill with 1 cup chopped parsley.

LOW-FAT OPTION:
➤ Use a canola oil to sauté the meatballs.

# TURKEY BREAST BAKED WITH ORANGE

*Serves 2–4.*

Replace the traditional holiday bird with this dish. I love the flavor of turkey with citrus.

| | |
|---|---|
| 2 tbsp | olive oil |
| 1 | small onion, chopped |
| 2 cloves | garlic, minced |
| 1/2 | sweet red pepper, chopped |
| 1/2 | sweet yellow pepper, chopped |
| 2 | celery stalks, chopped |
| 2 | boneless turkey breasts |
| 1 cup | fresh orange juice with pulp |
| 2 tbsp | orange zest |
| 1 tbsp | chopped fresh rosemary |
| 1 | bay leaf |
| 1/2 tsp | salt |
| 1/2 tsp | black pepper |
| 2 tbsp | Grand Marnier |
| 6 slices | orange |

SUGGESTED SIDE DISHES:
- Sweet potatoes with maple syrup and ginger
- Steamed carrots with lemon, chives and mint

In a large skillet, heat 1 tbsp of the oil. Gently sauté the onion and garlic until translucent. Add peppers and celery; sauté for 3–4 minutes. Remove and set aside. Heat remaining oil and sauté the turkey breasts gently for 10–15 minutes. Add in the orange juice, 1 tbsp of the orange zest, rosemary, bay leaf, salt, pepper and 1 tbsp of the Grand Marnier. Reduce heat to a simmer and poach, turning occasionally, 10–15 minutes until liquid has reduced. Transfer contents and reserved vegetables to baking dish and broil for about 5 minutes. Discard the bay leaf. Garnish with orange slices and remaining zest and Grand Marnier.

**PREPARATION TIME:**     *30-40 minutes*

VARIATIONS:
- Replace turkey with chicken breasts and reduce the cooking time slightly.
- Use grapefruit juice, zest and slices instead of orange.

LOW-FAT OPTIONS:
- Instead of sautéing the turkey, poach it in 1 cup orange juice.
- Replace the Grand Marnier with orange juice concentrate.

# TURKEY MEATBALL STROGANOFF WITH APPLE

*Serves 4.*

If you want a lighter version of this, combined with a lower fat content,
do as I did: replace the cream with non-fat yogurt or low-fat sour cream.

| | |
|---|---|
| 1 lb | lean ground turkey or chicken |
| 1 | small sweet red pepper, chopped |
| 1 | small onion, chopped |
| 2 cloves | garlic, chopped |
| 2 | eggs, beaten |
| 1/4 cup | dry bread crumbs |
| 1 cup | chopped parsley |
| 1 tbsp | balsamic vinegar |
| 1 tsp | light Worcestershire sauce |
| 4 tbsp | frozen apple juice concentrate, thawed |
| 1/2 tsp | salt |
| 1/2 tsp | black pepper |
| 1 tbsp | oil |
| 1 cup | chopped apple |
| 1/4 cup | apple juice |
| 1 cup | cream, low-fat yogurt or low-fat sour cream |
| 3 cups | egg noodles |

SUGGESTED SIDE DISHES:
- Borscht
- Salad with watercress, pears and nuts

*continued...*

# TURKEY MEATBALL STROGANOFF WITH APPLE
*continued*

In a bowl, mix together ground meat, red pepper, onion, garlic, eggs, bread crumbs, parsley, vinegar, Worcestershire sauce, 2 tbsp of the apple juice concentrate, salt and pepper; shape into 1-inch balls. In a large skillet, heat the oil and gently brown the meatballs, 4–6 minutes. Drain on paper towels. Drain off the oil and add remaining apple juice concentrate and apple pieces; just brown the apple. Add apple juice and yogurt. Lower heat and let thicken, stirring occasionally. Add meatballs and simmer another 10 minutes, occasionally checking the sauce. (If you use the low-fat yogurt, gently blend over lower heat, as yogurt has a lot of liquid.) Meanwhile, in a large pot of boiling water, cook egg noodles until tender but firm. Serve sauce over drained noodles.

**PREPARATION TIME:**     *20–25 minutes*

**TIME SAVER:**
Prepare the meatball mixture in a food processor.

VARIATIONS:
- Replace ground turkey with lean ground beef.
- Replace bread crumbs with quick-cooking oatmeal as a binding agent.
- Serve over rice or other types of pasta.

# Cajun Turkey Burgers

*Serves 2–4.*

These burgers are a delicious spicy variation on one of North America's favorite fast foods.

| | |
|---|---|
| 1 lb | lean ground turkey |
| 1/2 cup | diced sweet green pepper |
| 1/2 cup | diced sweet red pepper |
| 1/2 tsp | chopped jalapeño pepper (optional) |
| 1 | small onion, chopped |
| 1/2 cup | chopped fresh coriander |
| 2 cloves | garlic, chopped |
| 1/2 cup | dry bread crumbs |

**SUGGESTED SIDE DISHES:**
- Various types of bread
- Thin french fries

Mix all ingredients in a food processor or by hand. Shape into patties and broil or fry.

**PREPARATION TIME:**  *20–25 minutes*

VARIATIONS:
- Add Dijon mustard or Worcestershire sauce to the mixture.
- Replace coriander with fresh parsley.
- Add 1/2 tsp mild curry paste for more zest.

LOW-FAT OPTION:
- Grind your own turkey breast. This way you'll know the fat content, as sometimes ground turkey and chicken have the skin and fat mixed in.

# TURKEY SAUSAGE WITH SPICY TOMATO SAUCE

*Serves 2–4.*

Don't be intimidated by the title: this recipe involves a lot of chopping, not sausage-making. Serve with rice or slice the sausages and serve with the sauce over pasta.

| | |
|---|---|
| 4 | large turkey sausages |
| 1 tbsp | olive oil |
| 1 | small onion, chopped |
| 2 cloves | garlic, chopped |
| 1/2 cup | chopped celery |
| 1 | sweet green pepper, chopped |
| 1 | sweet red pepper, chopped |
| 1 tsp | chopped jalapeño pepper |
| 1/4 cup | chopped fennel |
| 1/4 cup | chopped fresh basil (or 1 tbsp dried) |
| 1 can | crushed tomatoes (19 oz/540 mL) |
| 1/4 tsp | salt |
| 1/2 tsp | black pepper |
| 1 | bay leaf |

SUGGESTED SIDE DISHES:
- Butternut squash soup
- Salad with goat cheese dressing
- Basmati rice with parsley and lentils

In a skillet, sauté the sausages in oil until brown. Remove sausages. In the same skillet, sauté the onions and garlic until translucent; add the celery, green and red peppers, jalapeño pepper, fennel, basil, tomatoes, salt, pepper and bay leaf. Cook the sausages for 3–5 minutes, then add to the tomato sauce. Reduce heat and simmer for 15–20 minutes until desired thickness. Discard the bay leaf.

**PREPARATION TIME:**   *20–25 minutes*

**TIME SAVER:**
Microwave the chopped vegetables; this will reduce the cooking time by about 5 minutes.

VARIATIONS:
- Use any other type of sausage.
- Replace fennel with celery.

LOW-FAT OPTIONS:
- Parboil the sausages to remove excess fat and then bake, instead of frying. If parboiling sausages, sauté the vegetables in low-sodium vegetable stock.
- Substitute this tomato sauce with Low-Fat Tomato Sauce (recipe on p. 26).

# MEATS

# CALVES' LIVER AND ONIONS EUROPEAN STYLE

*Serves 2–4.*

Liver and onions with mashed potatoes is something I have in my home
at least once a month.

| | |
|---|---|
| 2 tbsp | olive oil |
| 1 tbsp | butter |
| 2 | large Spanish onions, chopped |
| 1 lb | calves' liver |
| 2 cloves | garlic, minced |
| 1/4 cup | white wine |
| 1/2 tsp | salt |
| 1/2 tsp | black pepper |
| 1/4 cup | frozen apple juice concentrate, thawed |
| 1 tbsp | brown sugar or equivalent sweetener |
| 1/4 tsp | turmeric |
| 1/2 cup | chopped flat-leaf parsley |

SUGGESTED SIDE DISHES:
- Garlic mashed potatoes
- Stir-fried spinach with oranges

In a large skillet, heat 1 tbsp of the oil and the butter.
Sauté the onions until translucent. In a separate
skillet, heat remaining oil. Sauté the liver and garlic
for 5–7 minutes until the meat turns brown. Add the
white wine, salt and pepper. Reduce heat and simmer
another 5–7 minutes. To the onions, add the apple
juice concentrate, brown sugar and turmeric. Mix in
the parsley just before serving and then pour over the
liver.

**PREPARATION TIME:** *25–30 minutes*

VARIATION:
— Replace the calves' liver with chicken livers and reduce the cooking time.

LOW-FAT OPTIONS:
— Replace the butter and oil with a low-sodium vegetable stock and poach the vegetables and liver.
— Replace the white wine with apple or grape juice.

# STEAK WITH GREEN PEPPERCORN SAUCE

*Serves 2.*

This steak dish is a variation of a traditional recipe my father used to prepare on special occasions. You don't need a special occasion to try this, though.

| 2 | T-bone steaks, 2 inches thick |
|---|---|
| 1 tbsp | olive oil |
| 1/2 tsp | salt |
| 1/2 tsp | cracked black pepper |
| 1 tsp | dried rosemary |

### SAUCE:

| 1/2 cup | vegetable stock |
|---|---|
| 1/4 cup | milk |
| 1/4 cup | white wine |
| 1 tbsp | cognac |
| 1 tbsp | Dijon mustard |
| 1/4 cup | whipping cream OR |
| | 1/2 cup low-fat sour cream |
| 1 tsp | green peppercorns |

**SUGGESTED SIDE DISHES:**
- Fruity Strawberry Salad (recipe on p. 18)
- Brussels sprouts with almonds and lemon
- Baked spicy french fries

Pierce steaks with fork and trim excess fat. Brush both sides with olive oil. Sprinkle on salt, pepper and rosemary. Grill to perfection, about 5–6 minutes for rare, 7–8 minutes for medium.

### SAUCE:

In a saucepan, bring vegetable stock and milk to a boil. Reduce heat and allow mixture to reduce 3–5 minutes. Add wine and cognac; reduce another 3–5 minutes. Add mustard, cream and peppercorns. Reduce till sauce is a creamy consistency, about 3–5 minutes.

**PREPARATION TIME:**      *20–25 minutes*

**TIME SAVER:**
Make the sauce in advance and just gently heat it up while the steaks are grilling.

VARIATIONS:
- You can use a less-expensive cut of meat, but marinate it in red or white wine, covered and refrigerated, all day before cooking.
- Replace steak with tuna or swordfish.

LOW-FAT OPTIONS:
- Use skim milk or non-fat milk beverage instead of milk.
- Use low-fat sour cream instead of whipping cream.

# CAJUN-STYLE STEAK
*Serves 2.*

| | |
|---|---|
| 1 tsp | paprika |
| 1/2 tsp | onion powder |
| 1/2 tsp | garlic powder |
| 1/2 tsp | thyme |
| 1/2 tsp | cayenne pepper |
| 1/2 tsp | black pepper |
| 1/2 tsp | white pepper |
| 1/4 tsp | salt |
| 2 | small New York steaks |
| 1 tsp | olive oil |

**SAUCE:**

| | |
|---|---|
| 1 | sweet red pepper, chopped |
| 1 cup | mushrooms, chopped |
| 1 | small onion, chopped |
| 1 tsp | oil |
| 1/4 cup | apple juice |
| 1/4 cup | frozen apple juice concentrate, thawed |

**SUGGESTED SIDE DISHES:**
- Baked stuffed tomatoes
- Cream of Tomato Soup with Non-Fat Yogurt (recipe on p. 13)

In a bowl, combine paprika, onion powder, garlic powder, thyme, cayenne pepper, black pepper, white pepper and salt. Spread on wax paper. Coat both sides of the steaks.

**SAUCE:**

In a large skillet, heat 1 tsp oil and sauté red peppers, mushrooms and onion until translucent. Add apple juice and concentrate; reduce liquid by half. In a large skillet, sauté steaks in olive oil 5–6 minutes each side. Or, on your indoor grill, grill to desired doneness, about 5–6 minutes for rare, 7–8 minutes for medium. Spoon sauce over steaks.

**PREPARATION TIME:**     *25–30 minutes*

VARIATION:
— Replace New York steaks with small tenderloin steaks.

# GRILLED NEW YORK STEAK WITH HONEY, GARLIC AND GINGER

*Serves 2.*

I combined three of my favorite ingredients—honey, garlic and ginger—
to create a wonderful marinade for steak.

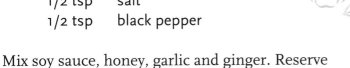

| | |
|---|---|
| 1/2 cup | light soy sauce |
| 1/4 cup | honey |
| 4 cloves | garlic, crushed |
| 1/2 tsp | chopped fresh ginger |
| 2 | New York steaks |

**SAUCE:**

| | |
|---|---|
| 1 tbsp | butter |
| 1 | large red onion, chopped |
| 1/2 cup | chopped sweet red pepper |
| 2 cups | sliced mushrooms |
| 1/2 tsp | salt |
| 1/2 tsp | black pepper |

**SUGGESTED SIDE DISHES:**
- Toasted herb bread
- Garlic mashed potatoes with olive oil and egg
- Green peas with mint

Mix soy sauce, honey, garlic and ginger. Reserve
1/4 cup of the mixture for basting. Marinate the steaks
10–15 minutes.

**SAUCE:**
Meanwhile, in a medium skillet, melt butter and sauté
the onions, red pepper and mushrooms until soft. Stir
in the salt and pepper. Keep the sauce warm. Grill
steaks, basting occasionally with marinade, 5–6 minutes
for rare, 7–8 minutes for medium. Pour sauce over
grilled steaks.

**VARIATION:**
— Instead of the New York
steak, use other types of
steak or boneless chicken
breasts.

**PREPARATION TIME:**     *25–30 minutes*

**TIME SAVER:**
Prepare the marinade a day in advance, allowing the
meat to soak up the wonderful flavors and be ready for
grilling at dinnertime. Be sure to refrigerate the meat,
covered.

**LOW-FAT OPTIONS:**
— Replace the honey with apple
juice concentrate.
— Replace the butter in the
sauce with vegetable stock.

# BEEF STEAK WITH MANGO SAUCE

*Serves 4.*

Beef Steak with Mango Sauce is another grill favorite. Mango's sweet flavor also goes well with poultry.

| | |
|---|---|
| 4 | New York strips or 4 T-bone steaks |
| 1-1/2 cups | mashed mango |
| 2 tsp | oil |
| 2 tsp | all-purpose flour |
| 3/4 cup | orange juice |
| 1/2 cup | chopped parsley |
| 1/2 tsp | salt |
| 1/2 cup | warm water |

**SUGGESTED SIDE DISHES:**
- Baked potatoes with dill
- Tomato salsa

Puncture both sides of each steak with a fork. Cover the top with 1/2 cup of the mashed mango and set aside. In a saucepan, heat the oil on medium heat. Gently stir in the flour (add some of the water if the roux is too thick). Stir for 2 minutes; do not brown. Then reduce heat to low. Add 1 cup of the mango, orange juice, half the chopped parsley, salt and water. Stir the sauce to prevent lumps and until it thickens. Keep sauce warm. Broil steaks, 5–6 minutes for rare, 7–8 minutes for medium. A minute before steak is done, spoon over some of the sauce. Place the steak on a serving plate with remainder of the sauce and sprinkle with remaining parsley.

**VARIATION:**
Replace the steak with a less-expensive cut, but marinate it longer, covered and refrigerated.

**LOW-FAT OPTIONS:**
Use very lean steak, such as tenderloin.
Use fish or poultry instead of steak.
Leave out the oil and flour; the sauce will be like a fruit relish.

**PREPARATION TIME:**     *25–30 minutes*

**TIME SAVER:**
Prepare the sauce in advance.
Start marinating the meat the night before and keep it covered and refrigerated until needed.

# BEEF TENDERLOIN FRIED IN SPICY TOMATO SAUCE

*Serves 4.*

This is a real meat lover's delight. I spice up this dish by adding more jalapeño peppers.

| | |
|---|---|
| 4 tbsp | olive oil |
| 4 | beef tenderloin steaks |
| 1 | medium onion, minced |
| 2 cloves | garlic, chopped |
| 1 can | crushed tomatoes (19 oz/540 mL) |
| 1 cup | red wine |
| 2 tbsp | chopped fresh rosemary (or 1 tsp dried) |
| 2 tbsp | chopped fresh oregano (or 1 tsp dried) |
| 1 tbsp | chopped flat-leaf parsley |
| 1/2 tsp | finely chopped jalapeño pepper OR 1 tsp hot sauce (both optional) |
| 1/2 tsp | salt |
| 1/2 tsp | black pepper |

**SUGGESTED SIDE DISHES:**
- Mashed potatoes with Parmesan cheese
- Carrots and sugar snap peas with mint and maple syrup

In a large skillet, heat 2 tbsp of the oil and sauté the steak 2–3 minutes on each side. Remove from pan and set aside. Add remaining oil to the pan and sauté the onion and garlic 2–3 minutes, being careful not to burn the garlic. Add the tomatoes, red wine, rosemary, oregano, parsley, jalapeño pepper, salt and pepper. Constantly stir and scrape any brown bits from the bottom of the pan for added flavor. Reduce heat and simmer the sauce for 10 minutes, stirring occasionally, till it is reduced by one-quarter. Return the steaks to the pan and cook for about 5 minutes, depending on degree of doneness desired. Turn the meat frequently to allow it to absorb the flavors of the sauce.

**PREPARATION TIME:**     *25–30 minutes*

**TIME SAVER:**
Chop the onions and garlic in a food processor.

VARIATION:
— Replace tenderloin with a less-expensive cut of beef, but marinate it in the morning with juice or wine. Keep covered and refrigerated until needed.

LOW-FAT OPTION:
— Sauté the vegetables and steaks in vegetable stock instead of oil.

# JUICY ORANGE BEEF

*Serves 2.*

This beef can be done under your broiler, on your indoor grill or on the barbecue in the summer. Mixing fruit and meat together has been done for centuries. Be adventurous!

| | |
|---|---|
| 1 | large orange (require rind and some sliced pieces and juice) |
| 1 tbsp | sugar or sweetener equivalent |
| 1/4 cup | soy sauce |
| 2 tsp | Worcestershire sauce |
| 1 tsp | chopped fresh oregano (or 1/2 tsp dried) |
| 1/2 tsp | salt |
| 1/2 tsp | black pepper |
| 2 | New York tenderloin steaks |

Remove 2 tbsp zest from the orange; set aside. Cut 6–8 thin slices from orange; set aside. Juice orange, reserving 1/2 cup juice. In a shallow pan, combine the orange juice, 1 tbsp of the orange zest, sugar, soy sauce, Worcestershire sauce, oregano, salt and pepper. Reserve 1/4 cup of the marinade for basting. Trim the fat off the steak. Punch holes on both sides with a fork, and marinate 10–15 minutes. Broil, grill or barbecue your steaks 5–6 minutes on each side for rare, 7–8 minutes for medium depending on thickness and cut, basting regularly with reserved marinade. One minute before serving, lightly grill orange slices. Transfer steaks to plates and garnish with grilled orange and remaining orange zest.

**PREPARATION TIME:**     *25–30 minutes*

**TIME SAVER:**

Prepare the marinade the night before and let the beef sit, covered and refrigerated. Not only will it be great tasting, it will be fast.

SUGGESTED SIDE DISHES:
- Noodles with broccoli, ginger and basil

TIPS:
➡ To keep fat and cholesterol levels down, limit yourself to a 3 oz serving of beef, and trim all excess fat off the meat.
➡ A good seedless orange for cooking is the navel. It is large, thick-skinned and very sweet and juicy.
➡ As soy sauce is high in sodium, look for low-sodium brands.

VARIATIONS:
➡ Use chicken instead of beef.
➡ Use a less-expensive cut of meat, but marinate it all day, covered and refrigerated, to achieve tenderness.

LOW-FAT OPTION:
➡ Use liquid sweetener rather than sugar.

# BOBOTIE

*Serves 4–6.*

Bobotie is a traditional Malay dish eaten by many South Africans. After the "Bobotie Show" aired, we received a large batch of letters from expatriate South Africans, who recounted fond memories. It's wonderful how food seems to do that.

| | |
|---|---|
| 1 slice | white bread |
| 1 cup | milk |
| 1 lb | lean ground beef |
| 2 tbsp | seedless grapes, minced |
| 1/2 cup | fruit chutney |
| 1 tbsp | mild curry paste (or 1/2 tbsp curry powder) |
| 1 | onion, chopped |
| 1/2 cup | chopped fresh apricots or sugarless apricot jam |
| 1/4 tsp | turmeric |
| 1/2 tsp | salt |
| 1/2 tsp | black pepper |
| 1 tbsp | lemon juice |
| 1 tbsp | vegetable or olive oil |
| 3 | eggs |
| 2 | bay leaves |

SUGGESTED SIDE DISHES:
- Saffron rice
- Tomato, onion and lettuce salad

*continued...*

# BOBOTIE
*continued*

Soak bread in 1/2 cup of the milk for 3–4 minutes. Squeeze out milk from bread and in a large bowl mix bread with the meat. Mix in grapes, chutney, curry paste, onion, apricots, turmeric, salt, pepper and lemon juice. In a large skillet, heat the oil. Sauté the beef mixture, stirring frequently, until brown. Transfer to 9- x 12-inch casserole dish. Beat remaining milk and eggs together and pour over the meat. Place the bay leaves on top of the mixture and bake, uncovered, at 375°F for 20–25 minutes until browned on top. Discard the bay leaves.

**PREPARATION TIME:**    *30–35 minutes*

**TIME SAVER:**
Prepare the mixture in advance and keep covered and refrigerated until needed.

VARIATIONS:
- Replace beef with lean ground chicken or turkey.
- Replace curry paste with 1 tsp of chopped fresh ginger.
- Replace chutney with unsweetened fruit (not apricot) jam.

LOW-FAT OPTIONS:
- Replace milk with skim milk or non-fat milk beverage.
- Drain oil after sautéing the meat mixture.

# THE PERFECT BURGER

*Serves 4–6.*

The purpose of the "Burger Show" was to demonstrate to our viewers how versatile hamburgers can be. The following two recipes include ingredients such as honey and condiments not usually applied to the backyard burger.

| | |
|---|---|
| 2 lb | lean ground beef |
| 1 | small onion, chopped |
| 1 clove | garlic, minced |
| 1 | egg, beaten |
| 1 tbsp | Worcestershire sauce |
| 1 tbsp | Dijon mustard |
| 1/2 cup | chopped parsley |
| 1 tbsp | honey |
| 1/2 tsp | salt |
| 1/2 tsp | black pepper |

**SUGGESTED SIDE DISHES:**
- Red potato salad
- Tomato salsa
- Grilled herbed mushrooms

In a bowl, mix together the beef, onion, garlic, egg, Worcestershire sauce, mustard, parsley, honey, salt and pepper. Shape into four or six patties. Grill or fry the patties 10–12 minutes. If grilling, oil the grill; if frying, dredge the patties in flour, then place in skillet with 2 tbsp hot oil.

**PREPARATION TIME:** *20–25 minutes*

**TIME SAVER:**
Use the food processor to blend the ingredients.

TIPS:
➤ For variety, use various types of hamburger buns, such as onion, 7-grain and cheese.
➤ For condiments and toppings, use different cheeses, onions, mustards, chutneys, salsas or tomato sauces.

VARIATIONS:
➤ Replace beef with lean ground turkey or chicken.
➤ For a great fish burger, replace beef with crab, tuna or swordfish. (Chop these up with the other ingredients.)

LOW-FAT OPTION:
➤ Use fish or seafood and broil the burgers.

# Cajun Burgers
*Serves 4–6.*

I love the simplicity of hamburgers, so I created this spicy version.
The coriander adds to the flavor of the jalapeño pepper and the meat.

| | |
|---|---|
| 2 lb | lean ground beef |
| 1/2 cup | chopped sweet green pepper |
| 1/2 cup | chopped sweet red pepper |
| 1 | large tomato, chopped |
| 1 | small onion, chopped |
| 2 cloves | garlic, minced |
| 1 | egg OR 1/4 cup non-fat yogurt |
| 1/2 cup | chopped fresh coriander |
| 1 tsp | chopped jalapeño pepper |
| 1/2 tsp | paprika |
| 1/2 tsp | salt |
| 1/2 tsp | black pepper |

SUGGESTED SIDE DISHES:
- Red potato salad
- Tomato salsa
- Grilled herbed mushrooms

In a large bowl, mix together ground beef, green and
red peppers, tomato, onion, garlic, egg, coriander,
jalapeño pepper, paprika, salt and pepper. Shape into
four patties. Grill or fry the patties. If grilling, oil the
grill; if frying, dredge the patties in flour, then place
in skillet with 2 tbsp hot oil.

**PREPARATION TIME:**     *20–25 minutes*

**TIME SAVER:**
Use the food processor to blend the ingredients.

VARIATION:
— Replace beef with lean
ground turkey or chicken.

LOW-FAT OPTION:
— Use fish or seafood and broil
the burgers.

# THREE THINGS YOU CAN DO TO MAKE GROUND MEAT INTERESTING

*Each serves 4–6.*

These three recipes are from the "Ground Meat Show"; try them for some new, delicious and economical variations on the standard fare.

### LEAN GROUND BEEF WITH TOMATOES AND HERBS ON TOASTED GARLIC BREAD

| | |
|---|---|
| 1 | small onion, chopped |
| 1 clove | garlic, minced |
| 1 tsp | olive oil |
| 1 lb | lean ground beef |
| 1/4 cup | chopped fresh basil |
| 1/2 tsp | salt |
| 1/2 tsp | black pepper |
| 1/2 tsp | paprika |
| 1/2 cup | canned red kidney beans |
| 1 | carrot, shredded |
| 2 | beefsteak tomatoes, chopped |
| 1 loaf | French or Italian bread |
| 2 tbsp | butter |
| 1/4 cup | chopped fresh dill |
| 2 cloves | garlic, minced |
| 2 | boiled eggs, finely chopped |

In a large skillet, sauté the onions and 1 clove garlic in olive oil. Add the beef, basil, salt, pepper, paprika, beans, carrot and tomatoes. Sauté until beef is cooked. Slice the loaf in half and toast it. Meanwhile, mix the butter, dill and 2 cloves garlic. Spread it on the toast. Spread cooked meat mixture over toast. Top with more freshly ground black pepper and the chopped egg.

*continued...*

# THREE THINGS YOU CAN DO TO MAKE GROUND MEAT INTERESTING

*continued*

## GROUND CHICKEN WITH CURRY AND PEAS
## WRAPPED IN A FLAT BREAD/TORTILLA

| | |
|---|---|
| 1 tsp | vegetable oil |
| 1 lb | lean ground chicken or turkey |
| 2 | shallots, chopped |
| 1/4 cup | chopped fennel |
| 1 tbsp | mild curry powder or paste |
| 1 tsp | minced fresh ginger |
| 1 tsp | sugar or sweetener equivalent |
| 1/2 tsp | lemon zest |
| 1/2 tsp | salt |
| 1/2 tsp | black pepper |
| 4 slices | lemon |
| 1/2 cup | watercress |
| 4 | flat breads or tortillas |

Heat oil in a large skillet and stir-fry chicken until partially cooked. Add the shallots, fennel, peas, coriander, curry powder, ginger, sugar, lemon zest, salt and pepper and cook another 3–4 minutes. Roll up mixture in flat bread or tortilla and garnish each with lemon slice and watercress.

# THREE THINGS YOU CAN DO TO MAKE GROUND MEAT INTERESTING
*continued*

## GROUND LAMB AND ROSEMARY IN PITA WITH NON-FAT YOGURT

| | |
|---|---|
| 1 tbsp | olive oil |
| 1 lb | ground lamb |
| 1/2 cup | pitted olives, chopped |
| 1 tsp | chopped fresh rosemary (or 1/2 tsp dried) |
| 1 tsp | chopped fresh oregano (or 1/2 tsp dried) |
| 1 clove | garlic, minced |
| 1 | small onion, chopped |
| 1/2 cup | chopped zucchini |
| 1/2 cup | chopped, oil-packed sun-dried tomatoes |
| 1/2 cup | crumbled feta cheese |
| 1/4 cup | dry white wine |
| 2 | pita bread |
| 4 tsp | non-fat yogurt |

In a large skillet, heat oil. Sauté the ground lamb until it turns brown. Add the olives, rosemary, oregano, garlic, onion, zucchini, tomatoes and wine. Reduce heat and simmer till liquid is reduced by one-quarter. Stir in the cheese. Place in pita bread, cut into wedges and garnish with a teaspoon of non-fat yogurt.

**PREPARATION TIME:** *25–30 minutes*

**TIME SAVER:**
Prepare the meat mixtures in advance; keep covered and refrigerated.

VARIATIONS:
- Mix and match any of the ground meats, keeping in mind that ground lamb has a flavor all its own.
- For vegetarian diets, replace the meat with white beans, chick peas or kidney beans.

LOW-FAT OPTION:
- Drain the excess oil or fat and use a nonstick pan.

# VEAL CHOPS BREADED WITH TARRAGON

*Serves 2–4.*

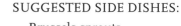

I tried a similar recipe for veal in Italy and decided to do this version with tarragon, which the French call the king of herbs. Tarragon, dried or fresh, will certainly add zest to any dish, especially when mixed with meat.

| | |
|---|---|
| 1/4 cup | dry bread crumbs |
| 1/2 tsp | garlic powder |
| 1 tsp | paprika |
| 1 tsp | chopped fresh tarragon (or 1/2 tsp dried) |
| 1/4 tsp | salt |
| 1/2 tsp | black pepper |
| 1 | large egg |
| 4 | lean veal chops |
| 1 tsp | butter |
| 1 tbsp | olive oil |

SUGGESTED SIDE DISHES:

- Brussels sprouts
- Potatoes with garlic and olive oil

In a shallow baking dish, mix together the bread crumbs, garlic powder, paprika, tarragon, salt and pepper. In a bowl, beat egg. Dip veal chops in egg, then coat in the bread crumb mixture, using a spoon to cover both sides. Over medium heat, heat butter and oil in a heavy skillet. Sauté chops about 4 minutes on each side until coating is golden. Make sure the heat is not so high that the coating sticks to the pan.

**PREPARATION TIME:**    *15–20 minutes*

TIPS:

- Although veal is lean, it's not fat-free and does contribute some cholesterol. Limit each portion to about 3 oz.
- You might want to soak the meat for half an hour in some milk before breading it. (This makes it easier to coat with the batter.)

VARIATIONS:

- Replace veal with pork chops or chicken pieces.
- Replace veal with cod or haddock. Tarragon goes very well with fish.

LOW-FAT OPTION:

- Instead of frying, bake the chops using vegetable spray to reduce the fat content.

# Veal Chops in Spicy Tomato Sauce with Peppers and Red Wine

*Serves 4.*

This quick and easy dinner always inspires lots of praise. The red wine adds a robust flavor.

| | |
|---|---|
| 4 | veal chops |
| 2 tbsp | olive oil |
| 2 | sweet red peppers, chopped |
| 4 | celery stalks, chopped |
| 1/2 cup | red wine |
| 1/4 cup | water |
| 1 tbsp | sugar OR 1/4 cup frozen apple juice concentrate, thawed |
| 1 tsp | dried basil |
| 1 tsp | dried rosemary |
| 1/2 tsp | chopped jalapeño pepper |
| 2 tbsp | soy sauce |
| 1 | bay leaf |
| 4 | large tomatoes, chopped |
| 1/2 tsp | salt |
| 1/2 tsp | black pepper |

SUGGESTED SIDE DISHES:
- Stir-fried spinach, onions and almonds
- Vegetable rice pilaf with lemon zest and juice
- Romaine salad with tofu dressing

In a large skillet, sauté the veal chops in the oil 2–4 minutes on each side; remove and set aside. To the skillet, add the peppers, celery, wine, water, sugar, basil, rosemary, hot peppers, soy sauce and bay leaf. Reduce heat and simmer 4–6 minutes. Add the veal and tomatoes and cook another 8–10 minutes or until veal is cooked through. Season with salt and pepper. Discard bay leaf. To serve, spoon sauce over chops.

**PREPARATION TIME:**     *25 minutes*

**TIME SAVER:**
Chop all the vegetables in the food processor. Use canned crushed or stewed tomatoes instead of fresh, and leave out the 1/4 cup of water.

VARIATION:
Replace the veal with pork chops or swordfish.

LOW-FAT OPTIONS:
Use half the oil.
Replace the red wine with grape juice.
Use a light soy sauce, which is lower in sodium.

# VEAL BROCHETTES WITH WHITE WINE AND ROSEMARY

*Serves 4–6.*

My friend Monica in Milan prepared these outstanding veal brochettes for me. I was amazed at how seemingly effortless the dish was to prepare.

| | |
|---|---|
| 1 | medium red onion |
| 2 lb | stewing veal |
| 2 tbsp | olive oil |
| 2 | shallots, chopped |
| 1 clove | garlic, chopped |
| 1/2 | sweet red pepper, chopped |
| 2 tbsp | chopped fresh rosemary |
| 1 tsp | lemon juice |
| 1/2 cup | dry white wine |
| 1/2 tsp | salt |
| 1/2 tsp | black pepper |

Cut the onion in four lengthwise and separate the slices. Thread veal and onion slices onto four to six 8-inch wooden skewers. In a large skillet, heat the oil. Gently sauté the shallots, garlic and red pepper 2–3 minutes. Add the brochettes and rosemary and sauté, turning constantly, 8–10 minutes until brochettes are browned. Add the lemon juice, wine, salt and pepper; reduce heat to low and simmer 7–10 minutes until brochettes turn white. Pour the sauce over top, then serve.

**PREPARATION TIME:** *25–30 minutes*

VARIATION:

Replace the veal with chicken pieces and increase cooking time slightly to ensure doneness.

LOW-FAT OPTION:

Replace the oil and wine with
1/2 cup apple or grape juice and poach rather than sauté the brochettes.

# New Zealand Spring Lamb with Rosemary and Wine

*Serves 2.*

The combination of herbs in this recipe brings out the fresh taste of the lamb, and I suggest two ways to prepare this dinner—grilling and sautéing. I first cooked this meal for friends in New Zealand. In New Zealand they know their lamb, and this recipe was a success. . . so I guess I passed the test!

| | |
|---|---|
| 3 cloves | garlic, minced |
| 2 | shallots, finely chopped |
| 1/4 cup | chopped fresh dill |
| 1 tbsp | dried rosemary |
| 2 tbsp | lemon juice |
| 1/2 cup | red wine |
| 1 | bay leaf |
| 1 | large sweet red pepper, chopped |
| 4 | large lamb chops OR 6 small 1-1/2-inch thick lamb chops |

SUGGESTED SIDE DISHES:
- Grilled new potatoes with sesame seeds and oil
- Green pea and mint soup
- Fruit salad
- Roasted potatoes
- Rice

## To Grill:

In a shallow baking dish, mix together the garlic, shallots, dill, rosemary, lemon juice, red wine and bay leaf. Remove 3 tbsp of the mixture and purée with the red pepper in a food processor. Reserve 1/2 cup of the purée mixture for garnish. Stir remaining purée into herb-wine mixture. Marinate lamb in a baking dish 10–15 minutes, turning occasionally. Grill lamb on both sides. Arrange on plates and garnish with reserved red pepper purée.

*continued...*

### To Sauté:

In a large skillet, gently sauté the lamb chops in 1 tbsp of olive oil 2–3 minutes each side. Add garlic, shallots, dill, rosemary, lemon juice, wine, bay leaf and red pepper. Reduce heat and simmer 5–8 minutes. Discard bay leaf.

**PREPARATION TIME:**     *20–25 minutes*

**TIME SAVER:**

Prepare the sauce or marinade in advance.

VARIATION:
— Replace the lamb with swordfish or tuna, and cook for a shorter time.

LOW-FAT OPTION:
— Before grilling, remove the fat from the lamb chops.

# LAMB CHOPS WITH ORANGE-YOGURT SAUCE

*Serves 2.*

Here is one of my favorite lamb recipes. I have combined orange and yogurt to create a tangy cream sauce.

| | |
|---|---|
| 2 tbsp | butter or olive oil |
| 4 | lamb chops, trimmed |
| 1 tsp | chopped fresh rosemary (or 1/2 tsp dried) |
| 1/2 tsp | salt |
| 1/2 tsp | black pepper |
| 1/4 cup | lemon juice |
| 2 | medium seedless oranges, peeled and chopped |
| 1/4 cup | orange juice |
| 2 tbsp | orange zest |
| 1/2 cup | low-fat yogurt or low-fat sour cream |
| | Orange slices for garnish |

**SUGGESTED SIDE DISHES:**
- Grilled eggplant and herbs
- Basmati rice with raisins and mild curry

In a large skillet, heat butter or oil. Sprinkle both sides of the lamb chops with rosemary, salt and pepper, and sauté the chops 4–6 minutes on each side, depending on how you like your meat done. Remove from pan and set aside. Lower heat to medium low and add the lemon juice, chopped orange, orange juice and half the orange zest. Reduce the mixture by half. Stir in the yogurt. Return the lamb to the pan for another 2 minutes, turning occasionally. Arrange chops on plates, spoon sauce over them, and garnish with the remaining orange zest and some orange slices.

**PREPARATION TIME:**       *25–30 minutes*

**VARIATIONS:**
- Replace lamb chops with veal or pork chops.
- Replace lamb chops with chicken breasts.
- Replace low-fat yogurt or low-fat sour cream with table cream.

**LOW-FAT OPTION:**
- Grill the lamb chops rather than sautéing them in oil.

# Lamb Chops with Cranberries

*Serves 2–3.*

In many meat dishes, I like to use several types of fruits and juices that are easily available at the local supermarket.

| | |
|---|---|
| 3/4 cup | unsweetened cranberry juice |
| 1/2 cup | red wine |
| 1 tbsp | red wine vinegar |
| 1 tbsp | lemon juice |
| 1 tbsp | olive oil |
| 1 | small onion, finely chopped |
| 2 cloves | garlic, crushed |
| 1 tbsp | chopped fresh thyme or rosemary (or 1/2 tsp dried) |
| 1/4 tsp | salt |
| 1/2 tsp | black pepper |
| 8 | 1-1/2–2-inch thick lamb chops |
| 1/4 cup | fresh or frozen cranberries for garnish |
| | Sprigs of fresh thyme for garnish |

In a shallow baking dish, combine cranberry juice, red wine, vinegar, lemon juice, oil, onion, garlic, chopped thyme, salt and pepper. Marinate lamb chops, covered and refrigerated, 20 minutes, turning occasionally, or longer if you have the time. Broil lamb chops basting occasionally with marinade, 5-8 minutes on each side, depending on how you like your meat done. Garnish with thyme sprigs and cranberries.

**PREPARATION TIME:**     *20–25 minutes*

SUGGESTED SIDE DISHES:
- Baby carrots
- Steamed asparagus

TIPS:
- Begin marinating meat the night before; the longer you marinate the better the flavor.
- Thicker lamb chops are more flavorful.
- If you don't remove fat from the lamb, the meat will have more flavor.

VARIATIONS:
- Replace the lamb with pork chops, and use a combination of apple juice or sauce and white wine.
- Replace the cranberry juice with apple juice and serve with grilled pieces of apple.

# BAKED LAMB CHOPS

*Serves 2.*

This dish allows you some free time while it is baking to spend with a friend. We call it "time-efficient" cooking.

| | |
|---|---|
| 4 | large lamb chops |
| 2 tbsp | olive oil |
| 3 cloves | garlic, minced |
| 2 | large onions, chopped |
| 4 | large carrots, chopped |
| 2 | sweet red peppers, chopped |
| 2 | tomatoes, chopped |
| 1 cup | chopped fresh spinach |
| 1/2 cup | frozen peas |
| 1/2 cup | pitted, sliced green olives |
| 1 cup | vegetable stock |
| 1 tsp | dried oregano |
| 1 tsp | dried thyme |
| 1 tsp | dried rosemary |
| 1/2 tsp | salt |
| 1 tsp | black pepper |

In a large skillet, gently sauté lamb chops in oil 3–4 minutes on each side. Transfer lamb to a medium-sized baking dish. Add the garlic, onions, carrots, red peppers, tomatoes, spinach, peas, olives and vegetable stock. Sprinkle with oregano, thyme, rosemary, salt and pepper. Bake, uncovered, at 400°F 20 minutes or until vegetables are done and lamb is cooked through.

**PREPARATION TIME:**  *30 minutes*

**TIME SAVER:**
Heat vegetable stock in the microwave to reduce cooking time by 5–7 minutes.

SUGGESTED SIDE DISHES:
- Chicken Rice Soup with Lemon (recipe on p. 9)
- Pita fried in pan and sprinkled with goat cheese and tomatoes

VARIATIONS:
- Use pork chops instead of lamb.
- Use lamb pieces and make a stew.
- Replace vegetable stock with same amount of puréed fresh or canned stewed tomatoes.

LOW-FAT OPTIONS:
- Cut some of the fat (not all of it, as it gives flavor) from the lamb.
- Instead of sautéing the lamb chops in oil, poach the chops in some of the vegetable stock.

# GRILLED PORK CHOPS WITH MUSTARD-PEACH SAUCE
*Serves 4.*

This is a different way to prepare pork chops—the peach sauce adds a light flavor to the pork.

| | |
|---|---|
| 4 | large pork chops |
| 4 tbsp | Dijon mustard |
| 2 tsp | butter |
| 1 tsp | mustard seeds |
| 1/2 cup | dry white wine |
| 1 cup | puréed fresh peaches |
| 1/2 cup | table or half-and-half cream |
| 1 tsp | dried mint |
| 1/2 tsp | salt |
| 1/2 tsp | black pepper |
| | Fresh peach slices for garnish |

SUGGESTED SIDE DISHES:
- Scalloped potatoes
- Salad
- Herbed vegetables steamed in vegetable stock

VARIATIONS:
- Replace the pork chops with veal chops or lamb.
- Replace the mint with tarragon.

LOW-FAT OPTIONS:
- Replace the cream with low-fat yogurt or low-fat sour cream.
- Replace the butter with a calorie-reduced margarine or low-fat butter.
- Replace the white wine with apple or grape juice.

Coat the pork chops with 2 tbsp of the mustard. Grill the chops, being careful not to overcook. Set aside and keep warm. In a small skillet, melt the butter and sauté the mustard seeds for 1 minute. Add the remaining mustard and wine. Simmer until reduced by half. Add the peaches, cream, mint, salt and pepper. Cook, stirring, until thickened; do not boil. Serve sauce over the chops, garnished with fresh peach slices.

**PREPARATION TIME:**     *25–30 minutes*

# CREAMY CURRY PORK CHOPS (DONE HEALTHY)

*Serves 2–4.*

Creamy Curry Pork Chops is a very economical recipe, one that my
parents often prepared when I was growing up. The curry adds bite to
this low-fat version.

| | |
|---|---|
| 1 tbsp | olive oil |
| 4 | lean pork chops or steaks |
| 1/2 cup | chopped fresh coriander |
| 1 | small onion (or 2 shallots), chopped |
| 1/2 cup | non-fat yogurt |
| 1 cup | low-fat sour cream |
| 1 tbsp | mild curry paste |
| | (or 1-1/2 tsp curry powder) |
| 1/4 tsp | salt |
| 1/2 tsp | black pepper |

**SUGGESTED SIDE DISHES:**
- Barbecued potatoes
- Glazed onions
- No-Mayo, No-Oil Caesar
  Salad (recipe on p. 20)

In a large skillet, heat the oil. Brown the pork chops
about 5 minutes on each side. Add half the coriander.
Transfer the pork to a baking dish just large enough to
hold the chops. In the skillet, brown the onion.
Reduce the heat to medium and add the yogurt, sour
cream, curry paste, remaining coriander, salt and
pepper. Cook, gently stirring sauce for 3–5 minutes
until it thickens. Pour the sauce over the pork and
bake, uncovered, at 375°F for 10 minutes.

**PREPARATION TIME:**     *25 minutes*

**TIPS:**
- Canadian pork is the leanest
  in the world and it is prized
  on the international market.
  To tenderize the meat, use a
  mallet.
- There are only 183 calories in
  1 cup of low-fat sour cream.

**VARIATION:**
- Replace pork chops with
  steak, chicken or swordfish.

# STIR-FRIED PORK WITH SNOW PEAS AND CARROTS

*Serves 4.*

Here's a very flavorful and colorful stir-fry.

| | |
|---|---|
| 2 tbsp | olive oil |
| 4 | boneless pork loin chops, cut into strips |
| 1 | onion, sliced |
| 2 cloves | garlic, minced |
| 4 | large carrots, sliced |
| 1 | sweet red pepper, chopped |
| 1 cup | snow peas |
| 1 | apple, sliced |
| 1/4 cup | frozen apple juice concentrate, thawed |
| 1 tsp | chopped fresh ginger |

In a wok or large skillet, heat the oil. Stir-fry the pork 4–6 minutes or until no longer pink inside. Add the onion and garlic. Stir-fry another 2 minutes or until the onions are translucent. Add the carrots and red pepper; stir-fry another 2 minutes. Do not overcook the vegetables. Add the snow peas, apple, apple juice concentrate and ginger. Toss well. Simmer another 2 minutes.

**PREPARATION TIME:**     *15–20 minutes*

**TIME SAVER:**
Slice the pork thinly and it will cook faster. Microwave to partially cook the carrots before stir-frying them.

SUGGESTED SIDE DISHES:
- Rice with dried fruit and spinach
- Salad with walnuts and Dijon vinaigrette
- Beefsteak tomatoes and broccoli with garlic

VARIATIONS:
- Replace pork with chicken.
- For a vegetarian meal, use tofu.
- Replace apple and apple juice with a pear and pear juice.

LOW-FAT OPTION:
- Use sliced chicken and stir-fry with vegetable stock rather than oil.

# MARINATED HAM STEAKS WITH APPLES

*Serves 4.*

This dish is quick, easy and economical—and a new way to use up left-over ham.

| | |
|---|---|
| 1/2 cup | applesauce |
| 1/4 cup | apple juice |
| 2 tsp | ground cloves |
| 1 tsp | paprika |
| 1 tsp | garlic powder |
| 1 tsp | dried parsley or chives |
| 4 | ham steaks, 1/2-inch thick |
| 2 | large apples, cut into quarters |

In a baking dish just large enough to hold the ham, combine applesauce, juice, cloves, paprika, garlic powder and parsley. Place ham in the mixture and marinate 10–15 minutes. Grill ham steaks with apple pieces, for 5–7 minutes, continuously basting ham with the marinade.

**PREPARATION TIME:**     *20–25 minutes*

**TIME SAVER:**
Make the marinade in advance.

VARIATIONS:
— Replace ham with shrimp or other seafood.
— Replace the apples with peaches or nectarines.
— Bake the ham at 350°F for 10–12 minutes, occasionally basting with the marinade.

LOW-FAT OPTION:
— Choose a low-sodium ham with very little fat.

# HAM WITH PEACHES AND BANANAS

*Serves 2–4.*

This is a great recipe for leftover holiday ham. Try to buy fresh, not
processed, ham: it is lower in sodium.

| | |
|---|---|
| 1 tbsp | butter, melted |
| 1/2 tsp | cinnamon |
| 1/2 tsp | curry powder |
| | Juice of half a lemon |
| 1 tbsp | brown sugar |
| 1/4 cup | chopped fresh coriander |
| 2 | cooked ham steaks |
| 2 | bananas |
| 2 | peaches OR 1 can unsweetened |
| | peaches (19 oz/540 mL), drained |

In a bowl, combine butter, cinnamon, curry powder,
lemon juice, sugar and coriander. Place ham steaks in
a baking dish just large enough to hold them. Slice the
bananas lengthwise and the peaches in eighths.
Arrange on top of the ham and pour sauce over. Bake,
uncovered, at 400°F 8–10 minutes or until brown.

**PREPARATION TIME:**     *20 minutes*

**TIME SAVER:**
Marinate the ham overnight.

VARIATIONS:
- You can also use pears,
  apples, nectarines or raisins.
- Replace the brown sugar
  with maple syrup.

LOW-FAT OPTION:
- Instead of brown sugar, use
  a liquid sweetener or 1/4 cup
  apple juice concentrate.

# HAM WITH PINEAPPLE, OUZO AND GRAPES

*Serves 2–4.*

| | |
|---|---|
| 1/4 cup | ouzo |
| 2 tbsp | unsweetened pineapple juice |
| 1 tbsp | frozen grape or apple juice concentrate, thawed |
| 1/2 tsp | dried oregano |
| 1/4 tsp | ground cloves |
| 2 | cooked ham steaks |
| 4 | fresh or canned unsweetened pineapple rings |
| 1 cup | green or red seedless grapes |

**SUGGESTED SIDE DISHES:**
- Greek salad
- Grilled or fried pita bread

In a baking dish just large enough to hold the ham steaks, combine the ouzo, pineapple juice, grape juice concentrate, oregano and cloves. Place ham steaks in dish and garnish with the pineapple rings and grapes. Bake, uncovered, at 375°F for 8–10 minutes until pineapple rings start to turn a brownish color.

**PREPARATION TIME:**     *15–20 minutes*

**TIME SAVER:**
Marinate the ham in advance.

VARIATION:
— Replace the brown sugar with maple syrup.

LOW-FAT OPTION:
— Replace the brown sugar with a liquid sweetener or 1 tbsp of apple juice concentrate.

# ROASTED ITALIAN SAUSAGE WITH PEPPERS AND RICE

*Serves 4.*

This is a very well-balanced, hearty dinner. Experiment with different types of sausages, as well as with vegetables.

| | |
|---|---|
| 4 | hot Italian sausages |
| 2 tbsp | vegetable or olive oil |
| 2 | medium onions, chopped |
| 2 cloves | garlic, minced |
| 2 | sweet red peppers, chopped |
| 2 | sweet green peppers, chopped |
| 1/2 cup | chopped fennel |
| 1 cup | sliced mushrooms |
| 1 cup | rice |
| 1 cup | shredded fresh spinach |
| 1 tsp | dried basil |
| 1 tsp | dried tarragon |
| 1/2 tsp | salt |
| 1/2 tsp | black pepper |
| 2 cups | hot vegetable stock |

SUGGESTED SIDE DISHES:
- Toasted Italian bread with rosemary and feta cheese
- Cream of Tomato Soup with Non-Fat Yogurt (recipe on p. 13)
- Leaf lettuce salad with sliced pears

In a large skillet, brown the sausages in oil; remove and set aside. In the same skillet, sauté the onions and garlic for about 2 minutes, until translucent. Add the red and green peppers, fennel, mushrooms and rice, and sauté 2 minutes. Add the spinach, basil, tarragon, salt, pepper and hot vegetable stock; cook 5 minutes. Pour contents into a casserole dish. Arrange the sausages on top. Bake, covered, at 375°F for 15 minutes or until the rice is cooked.

**PREPARATION TIME:**     *25–30 minutes*

**TIME SAVER:**
Use a food processor to chop the vegetables.

VARIATIONS:
— Replace the hot sausage with turkey or chicken sausages.
— Replace the sausage with large tiger shrimp.

LOW-FAT OPTIONS:
— Boil the sausages, rather than sautéing them, to remove excess fat.
— Use lower-fat sausages such as veal, chicken and turkey.

# ONE-POT MEALS

I am a "special needs" ten-year-old boy and my mom is helping me write this letter. I want you to know how much I like watching your show—sometimes my dad and sisters watch your show with me.

My mom and I just finished watching you make beef brochettes, spaghetti squash, broccoli, pear and bacon stir fry, and potatoes with herbs.

If you are ever in Edmonton, I would love for you to come to my house for dinner. We could all cook together in my kitchen. Please write me if you have the time.

Thanks so much,

*Michael*
Edmonton

# FLORENTINE HAM AND POTATO CASSEROLE
*Serves 4–6.*

| | |
|---|---|
| 2 cups | chopped cooked ham |
| 1 cup | shredded fresh spinach |
| 1/2 cup | diced sweet red pepper |
| 1 | large onion, chopped |
| 1 cup | shredded cheddar cheese |
| 1/2 cup | non-fat yogurt |
| 1/2 cup | milk |
| 4 | eggs, beaten |
| 1/2 tsp | paprika |
| 4 | large potatoes, sliced |
| 1/2 cup | shredded mozzarella cheese |

SUGGESTED SIDE DISHES:
- Waldorf salad
- Vegetable soup

In a bowl, mix well the ham, spinach, red pepper, onion, cheddar cheese, yogurt, milk, eggs and paprika. Line the bottom and sides of a nonstick or lightly oiled large baking dish with potato slices. Sprinkle half the mozzarella cheese on the potatoes. Spoon in the ham filling. Bake, uncovered, at 375°F for 20–25 minutes. Sprinkle with remaining mozzarella and bake another 5 minutes until brown.

**PREPARATION TIME:**     *30–35 minutes*

LOW-FAT OPTIONS:
—— Replace cheeses with low-fat and skim-milk cheeses.
—— Replace ham with cooked skinless pieces of cubed chicken.

# MEDLEY OF STEWED/ROASTED MEAT AND VEGETABLES IN WINE

*Serves 6–8.*

This medley in wine is a great combination of meat flavors. I sometimes prepare this recipe with rice and also add hot peppers. If you want, try both versions—and let me know what you think.

| | |
|---|---|
| 4 | chicken pieces |
| 1 lb | beef steak |
| 4 | small Italian sausages |
| 1 tbsp | olive oil |
| 1 cup | baby carrots |
| 1 cup | pearl onions |
| 1 cup | small potatoes, chopped |
| 1/2 cup | chopped fennel |
| 4 cloves | garlic, chopped |
| 1 | medium red onion, chopped |
| 1 tbsp | chopped fresh tarragon |
| 1 tbsp | chopped fresh basil |
| 1 tsp | chopped fresh sage |
| 2 | bay leaves |
| 4 cups | chicken or beef stock |
| 1/2 cup | white wine |
| 2 cups | canned white kidney beans |
| 4 | tomatoes, chopped |

SUGGESTED SIDE DISHES:
- Mixed green salad
- Lentil soup

*continued...*

# MEDLEY OF STEWED/ROASTED MEAT AND VEGETABLES IN WINE

*continued*

Cut chicken, steak and sausage into bite-sized pieces. In a heavy casserole dish, heat oil and sauté meats 8–10 minutes until brown. (Or sauté meats in a large skillet and transfer to a crock pot.) Add carrots, pearl onions, potatoes, fennel, garlic, red onion, tarragon, basil, sage, bay leaves, chicken stock and white wine. Bring to a boil. Reduce the heat to low and simmer, uncovered, 20–25 minutes (or bake, covered, at 375°F for 15–20 minutes), until meat is completely cooked. Add the beans and tomatoes; simmer (or bake) another 5–10 minutes until tomatoes are cooked. Discard the bay leaves.

**PREPARATION TIME:** *35–40 minutes*

VARIATIONS:
- Replace any of the red meat with veal, pork or lamb.
- Replace the Italian sausages with other sausages such as turkey, veal or pork.

LOW-FAT OPTION:
- Microwave the meat and drain the excess fat. Make sure to remove the skin and fat from the chicken and prick holes in the sausage.

# QUICK BEEF STEW
*Serves 6–8.*

This beef stew is a healthy one-pot meal, and most of the work is in the chopping. The gem is you can freeze this and reheat it later in the microwave.

| | | SUGGESTED SIDE DISHES: |
|---|---|---|
| 2 tbsp | olive oil | • Four-bean salad |
| 2 lb | good-quality stewing beef | • Cream of cauliflower soup |
| 1 | large onion, chopped | with curry |
| 1 | large carrot, chopped | • Garlic bread |
| 1 | small turnip or squash, chopped | |
| 2 | celery stalks, chopped | |
| 1/2 | sweet red pepper, chopped | |
| 1/2 | sweet green pepper, chopped | |
| 1 | small zucchini, chopped | |
| 2 | medium potatoes, chopped | |
| 2 cups | beef stock | |
| 2 cups | dry red wine | |
| 1 tsp | dried basil | |
| 1 tsp | dried oregano | |
| 1/2 tsp | salt | |
| 1 tsp | black pepper | |
| 1 | bay leaf | |
| | All-purpose flour (if desired to thicken) | |

*continued...*

# QUICK BEEF STEW

*continued*

In a crock pot, slow cooker or large deep saucepan, heat the oil and sauté the beef 3–5 minutes until brown. Add the onion, carrot, turnip, celery, red and green peppers and zucchini; sauté for another 5 minutes. Meanwhile, microwave the potatoes till tender, about 3 minutes at High. Add the potatoes to the stew along with the stock, wine, basil, oregano, salt, pepper and bay leaf. Bring the stew to the boil; reduce the heat and simmer, uncovered, 20–25 minutes. Do not overcook the vegetables. Discard the bay leaf. When thickening with flour, take 1 tbsp flour, add 1/4 cup cold water and mix. Add to mixture.

**PREPARATION TIME:**     *30–40 minutes*

**TIME SAVER:**

Microwave the carrots and turnip to reduce the cooking time by 8–10 minutes.

VARIATION:

Replace the beef with poultry and replace beef stock with chicken stock.

LOW-FAT OPTION:

To make a vegetarian stew, replace meat with tofu, add more vegetables and use a vegetable stock.

# BEEF STEW MADE QUICK AND EASY WITH THE HELP OF A MICROWAVE

*Serves 6.*

The most time-consuming thing in this recipe is the chopping, but all of the preparation will be worth it when you take your first bite.

| | |
|---|---|
| 2 tbsp | vegetable or olive oil |
| 1 cup | baby onions OR |
| | 1 medium onion, chopped |
| 4 | celery stalks, chopped |
| 2 lb | stewing beef |
| 4 | medium potatoes, cubed |
| 1 | small turnip OR |
| | 1 medium rutabaga, chopped |
| 2 | large carrots, coarsely chopped |
| 1 | sweet red pepper, chopped |
| 1 | sweet green pepper, chopped |
| 1 | small zucchini, chopped |
| 1 | bay leaf |
| 1 tsp | dried basil |
| 1 tsp | dried oregano |
| 1/2 tsp | salt |
| 1/2 tsp | black pepper |
| 2 cups | beef stock |
| 1 cup | dry red wine |

SUGGESTED SIDE DISHES:
- Carrot and ginger soup
- Asparagus with tarragon vinaigrette

*continued...*

# BEEF STEW MADE QUICK AND EASY WITH THE HELP OF A MICROWAVE
### *continued*

In a crock pot or heavy saucepan, heat the oil and sauté baby onions and celery 1 minute or until starting to brown. Add beef and cook for 5–7 minutes until brown. Microwave potatoes, turnips and carrots on High 4 minutes. Add potatoes, turnip, carrots, red and green peppers, zucchini, bay leaf, basil, oregano, salt, pepper, chicken stock and red wine. Simmer, uncovered, 15–20 minutes. Discard the bay leaf.

**PREPARATION TIME:** *30–35 minutes*

**TIME SAVER:**

Use the food processor to chop the vegetables. Cut the beef cubes smaller so they cook faster.

VARIATIONS:
— Replace stewing beef with veal or lamb.
— Replace basil with rosemary, especially if you are using lamb.
— Substitute grape juice or apple juice for the red wine.

LOW-FAT OPTIONS:
— Use a very lean cut of stewing beef.
— Replace the beef with cubed skinless chicken breasts.

# PORK STEW WITH TOMATO AND OLIVES

*Serves 6–8.*

The olives add flair to this traditional pork stew; I remember once my guests commenting how unusual but flavorful this meal was. In my kitchen and on "What's for Dinner?" I encourage experimentation. A bonus is that this dinner is relatively inexpensive.

| | |
|---|---|
| 1/2 lb | bacon, chopped |
| 1 | large red onion, chopped |
| 3 cloves | garlic, minced |
| 3 lb | boneless pork, cut into 1-inch pieces |
| 1 can | tomatoes (19 oz/540 mL) |
| 1 cup | white wine |
| 1 cup | meat or vegetable stock |
| 1 tsp | dried sage |
| 1 tsp | dried oregano |
| 1/2 tsp | salt |
| 1/2 tsp | black pepper |
| 1 | bay leaf |
| 1 cup | pitted black olives, chopped |

**SUGGESTED SIDE DISHES:**
- Roasted garlic potatoes with rosemary
- Sautéed baby onions and carrots with mint and tarragon
- Cabbage salad with citrus dressing

In a large heavy saucepan, fry the bacon until tender, not crisp. Add the onions, garlic and pork. Sauté 8–10 minutes. Add the tomatoes, white wine, stock, sage, oregano, salt, pepper and bay leaf. Bring to a boil. Reduce the heat and simmer, uncovered, 15–20 minutes. Add the black olives. Simmer 5 more minutes. Discard the bay leaf.

**PREPARATION TIME:**     *30–35 minutes*

VARIATIONS:
- Replace the pork with lean stewing beef or lean stewing lamb.
- Replace the white wine with red wine or grape juice.

LOW-FAT OPTIONS:
- Use lean boneless pork.
- Leave out the bacon and sauté onions garlic and pork with 1 tsp of vegetable oil.
- Choose a vegetable stock that is low in sodium and contains no MSG.
- Replace the olives with mushrooms.

# SEAFOOD STEW IN RICE

*Serves 6–8.*

This seafood stew is not only delicious but very healthy and gives you plenty of options to use whatever is in your kitchen. On "What's for Dinner?" we tell our viewers to look in their cupboards and refrigerators and use what they already have, even if it means replacing some ingredients. This was the episode when my friend Brian Orser came on the show to assist us. Mary Jo and I did a Tonya Harding and Nancy Kerrigan routine. Oh boy!

| | |
|---|---|
| 2 tbsp | olive oil |
| 1 lb | squid, cut into rings |
| 1 | medium onion, chopped |
| 2 cloves | garlic, minced |
| 2 | carrots, chopped |
| 1 | small zucchini, chopped |
| 1 cup | rice |
| 2 cups | boiling vegetable stock |
| 1/2 cup | dry white wine |
| 2 | large tomatoes, chopped |
| 1 | sweet red pepper, chopped |
| 1/2 cup | chopped fennel |
| 1 tbsp | dried tarragon |
| 1 tsp | dried basil |
| 1/2 tsp | turmeric |
| 1/2 tsp | salt |
| 1/2 tsp | black pepper |
| 1/4 tsp | saffron |
| 1 | bay leaf |
| 1 | tuna steak, cubed |
| 1 | swordfish steak, cubed |
| 1 lb | large jumbo shrimp |
| 1 lb | mussels |

SUGGESTED SIDE DISHES:
- Creamy sweet pepper soup
- Leaf lettuce with mango dressing

# SEAFOOD STEW IN RICE
*continued*

In a large heavy saucepan, heat the oil. Sauté the squid 3–5 minutes until it turns white and begins to curl. Add onion, garlic, carrots and zucchini. Cook 2–3 minutes. Add the rice, boiling stock, white wine, tomatoes, red pepper, fennel, tarragon, basil, turmeric, salt, pepper, saffron and bay leaf. Bring to a boil; reduce heat and simmer 10 minutes until liquid is reduced by half. Add the tuna, swordfish, shrimp and mussels. Cover and cook over medium heat till rice is done and mussels open, 20–25 minutes. Discard the bay leaf and any mussels that do not open.

**PREPARATION TIME:**     *30–35 minutes*

**TIME SAVER:**
Microwave the firmer vegetables such as carrots and fennel; this will save 8–10 minutes in cooking time. Microwave the soup stock while chopping the vegetables and seafood.

VARIATION:
—— Replace the fennel with celery.

LOW-FAT OPTION:
—— Leave out the oil and sauté the squid, onion, garlic, carrots and zucchini in soup stock.

# CHILI WITH LEAN GROUND BEEF
*Serves 6–8.*

On the show we served this chili over rice, but you could serve it over pasta also. Mary Jo decided to throw in some extra vegetables we had in the refrigerator, and it resulted in a very tasty and economical one-pot meal.

| | |
|---|---|
| 1 tbsp | olive oil |
| 1 lb | lean ground beef |
| 1 | large onion, chopped |
| 1 clove | garlic, minced |
| 1 | sweet green pepper, chopped |
| 1 | sweet red pepper, chopped |
| 1/2 cup | chopped celery |
| 1 can | stewed tomatoes (28 oz/796 mL) |
| 1 can | red kidney beans (19 oz/540 mL) |
| 3/4 cup | chopped fresh dill or parsley |
| 1/2 cup | apple juice |
| 1 tbsp | chili powder |
| 1/2 tsp | chopped jalapeño pepper OR |
| | 1 tsp hot sauce |
| 1/2 tsp | salt |
| 1/2 tsp | black pepper |
| 2 tbsp | tomato paste |

In crock pot or large heavy saucepan, heat oil and brown ground beef 5–7 minutes. Make a well in center of meat and add onions, garlic, green and red pepper and celery. Sauté until the onions are translucent. Stir in tomatoes, kidney beans, dill, apple juice, chili powder, jalapeño pepper, salt, pepper and tomato paste. Simmer, uncovered and stirring occasionally, for 20 minutes.

**PREPARATION TIME:**     *25–30 minutes*

SUGGESTED SIDE DISHES:
- Rice with chick peas
- Salad

TIPS:

➤ The word "chili" is derived from the Greek word that translates into "I bite."

➤ Chili shifts your metabolism into high gear, which keeps you slim and even helps relieve gas. It does not promote stomach distress or ulcers.

➤ Cook (or thaw) your lean ground beef by microwaving it. This zaps more fat from it than broiling.

➤ To help introduce your kids to spicy food, let them know that milk—not water—cools the mouth down after a hot meal. Bread works too!

VARIATIONS:

➤ For a vegetarian chili, replace meat with tofu.

➤ Replace beef with ground chicken or turkey.

LOW-FAT OPTION:

➤ After the beef is cooked, drain it on a paper towel to soak up the excess fat.

# CURRY MEATLOAF WITH YOGURT AND DILL

*Serves 6.*

This meatloaf is comfort food to soothe the soul—a hearty meal for a cool fall night. I slice the meatloaf and serve open-faced sandwiches—if there's any left over!

| | |
|---|---|
| 2 lb | lean ground beef |
| 1 | egg |
| 1 | small onion, chopped |
| 2 cloves | garlic, minced |
| 1 | sweet red or green pepper, chopped |
| 1/2 cup | dry bread crumbs |
| 1/2 cup | chopped fresh dill |
| 1/4 cup | chopped fresh coriander (optional) |
| 1/2 cup | low-fat yogurt or low-fat sour cream |
| 2 tbsp | curry paste (or 1 tbsp powder) |
| 1 tsp | dried tarragon |
| 1/2 tsp | salt |
| 1/2 tsp | black pepper |

SUGGESTED SIDE DISHES:

- Rice with bananas, peas and spinach
- Asparagus with butter and mint
- Parsley and tomato salad

In a large bowl, combine ground beef, egg, onion, garlic, red pepper, bread crumbs, dill, coriander, yogurt, curry paste, tarragon, salt and pepper. Mix well and turn into a 9- x 4-inch baking dish. Bake at 350°F for 25–30 minutes until meatloaf is done in the center and browned on top.

**PREPARATION TIME:**     *30 minutes*

**TIME SAVER:**
Use a food processor to mix the vegetables and herbs.

VARIATIONS:
- Substitute lean ground turkey or chicken for the beef.
- Replace beef with tofu to make a vegetarian meal.

LOW-FAT OPTION:
- Use low- or non-fat yogurt and *extra*-lean ground beef.

# HAM, CHEESE AND CURRY EGG PIE

*Serves 2–4.*

| | |
|---|---|
| 4–6 | eggs |
| 1 cup | chopped cooked ham |
| 1 cup | shredded cheddar or skim-milk mozzarella cheese |
| 2 | small shallots (or 1 onion), chopped |
| 1/4 cup | chopped fresh coriander or flat-leaf parsley |
| 1/2 cup | non-fat yogurt OR 1/4 cup low-fat sour cream |
| 1 tbsp | curry paste (or 1 tsp powder) |
| 1/4 tsp | salt |
| 1/4 tsp | black pepper |
| 1/4 cup | grated Parmesan cheese |

In a large bowl, mix together the eggs, ham, cheddar, shallots, coriander, yogurt, curry paste, salt and pepper. Spray a large baking dish with a nonstick vegetable spray and pour in the egg mixture. Bake, uncovered, at 350°F for 15 minutes, checking to make sure it does not burn. Sprinkle with the Parmesan cheese and bake 5 more minutes.

**PREPARATION TIME:**     *20–25 minutes*

VARIATIONS:
- Replace cheese with soft tofu.
- Replace coriander with fresh parsley.

LOW-FAT OPTION:
- Replace the ham with skinless cooked chicken breast.

# TURKEY SHEPHERD'S PIE

*Serves 6.*

This is a very nutritious meal that everyone will enjoy, and it doesn't have to take a long time to prepare—just be organized. On this episode, the mixer I was using to mash the potatoes wouldn't shut off; Mary Jo had to rescue me!

| | |
|---|---|
| 6–8 | potatoes |
| 1/2 cup | low-fat yogurt OR 2 tbsp butter |
| 1/2 cup | milk |
| 1/2 cup | chopped fresh dill |
| 1 tsp | vegetable oil |
| 1 | small onion, chopped |
| 1/2 lb | lean ground turkey |
| 1 cup | diced carrots |
| 1 cup | frozen peas |
| 1/2 cup | diced celery |
| 1/2 cup | diced green pepper |
| 2 cloves | garlic, chopped |
| 1 tsp | dried sage |
| 1/2 tsp | salt |
| 1/2 tsp | black pepper |
| 1/4 cup | grated Parmesan cheese |

SUGGESTED SIDE DISHES:
- Tomato basil cream soup
- Spinach salad with feta and bacon
- Flatbread with herbs, red onion and goat cheese

Boil potatoes and mash them with yogurt, milk and dill. In a large skillet, heat the oil. Sauté the onion until translucent. Add the ground turkey. Cook 5–6 minutes until brown. Add the carrots, peas, celery, green pepper, garlic, sage, salt and pepper; cook for 2 minutes. In a large, deep, nonstick baking dish, make a layer of one-third of the mashed potatoes, then half of the meat mixture, then half of the peas. Repeat, finishing with potato mixture. Sprinkle on the Parmesan cheese. Bake, uncovered, at 350°F for 10–15 minutes until brown on top.

**PREPARATION TIME:** *30 minutes*

**TIME SAVER:**
Cook potatoes in the microwave, then mash.

VARIATION:
— Replace turkey with lean ground beef.

LOW-FAT OPTIONS:
— Instead of yogurt or butter, mash the potatoes with some of the potato water or low-fat sour cream.
— Drain your turkey meat of all the oil before adding the vegetables.

I wish to thank you for a very enjoyable, informative program. Although I myself am already an experienced hobby cook, I thoroughly enjoy your type of cooking because it replicates my style: lots of vegetables, low in fat, low in animal protien, no frying, little baking, good use of microwave and other energy-saving appliances, appealing presentations, etc.

I was so enthralled with your grill I was determined to find one like yours.

You will be pleased to hear that your program is the only show I look at, on any of the channels. You have even replaced Lloyd Robertson on the CTV News, which I normally watched around 11pm. Now that I am hooked on your show, I hardly get to listen/see Lloyd.

There is a nice touch of the unexpected whenever Ken's mother drops by, or there's a visit by Ruby, etc....

I have so many recipes I would like to request that it would be easier if you had a cookbook ... in the meantime, here goes: Stuffed Calamari, Curried Chicken Meatloaf, Cajun Meatloaf, Quick and Easy Coq au Vin....


Thanks very much, and continue the good work,


*Judy*
Ottawa

# FISH AND SHELLFISH

# GRILLED SEAFOOD AND VEGETABLES
*Serves 4–6.*

I like to prepare this recipe with whatever seafood is available at the time. Choose seafood that is firm and will not fall apart on the grill.

| | |
|---|---|
| 1 lb | tuna steak |
| 1 lb | swordfish |
| 1 lb | jumbo prawns OR |
| | 1 lobster tail, sliced |
| 1 | small red onion |
| 1 | sweet red pepper |
| 1 | zucchini |
| 2 | carrots |
| 2 tbsp | lemon juice |
| 1 tbsp | olive oil |
| 3 tbsp | chopped fresh oregano |
| 2 tbsp | chopped fresh tarragon |
| 1/2 tsp | salt |
| 1/2 tsp | black pepper |
| 3 cups | watercress |
| 2 | lemons, cut in wedges |

SUGGESTED SIDE DISHES:
- Pasta with garlic and olive oil
- Sliced tomatoes with mint and olive oil

Soak six 8-inch wooden skewers. Cut into 2-inch pieces the tuna, swordfish and prawns. Cut onion, red pepper and zucchini into 1-inch chunks. Thickly slice carrots diagonally. In a large bowl, mix the lemon juice, olive oil, oregano, tarragon, salt and pepper. Fold in the vegetables and seafood. Thread vegetables and seafood onto skewers. Grill until seafood lightens in color and vegetables are tender. Serve brochettes on a bed of watercress with grilled lemon wedges.

**PREPARATION TIME:**     *25–30 minutes*

**TIME SAVER:**
Microwave the carrots and zucchini to partly cook them first. Cut the seafood in cubes and marinate in lemon juice several hours ahead.

VARIATIONS:
- Replace the tuna with salmon.
- For vegetarian diets, replace all the seafood with a varied selection of firm vegetables.
- For meat lovers, replace the seafood with chicken, sausage and cubed steak.

# POACHED STUFFED SOLE IN WHITE WINE AND MINT

*Serves 4.*

Poaching in white wine and mint adds marvelous flavor, aroma and color. It is also healthy and fairly low in fat.

| | |
|---|---|
| 1 tsp | vegetable or olive oil |
| 1/2 cup | chopped shallots or onions |
| 1 cup | white wine |
| 1 cup | water |
| 1/2 cup | chopped fresh mint |
| 1/2 tsp | salt |
| 1 tsp | black pepper |
| 1 | bay leaf |
| 4 | sole fillets |
| 1 cup | chopped fresh spinach |
| 8 | jumbo shrimp, tail on |

SUGGESTED SIDE DISHES:
- Steamed vegetables with mint
- Stuffed tomatoes
- Grilled zucchini with rosemary and olive oil

In a skillet or sauté pan, heat the oil and sauté the shallots for 2 minutes or until translucent. Add the wine, water, mint, half of the salt, half of the pepper and the bay leaf. Bring to a boil; immediately reduce the heat and simmer 5 minutes. Sprinkle the fish with the remaining salt and pepper. Place spinach on each fillet; arrange two shrimp cross-wise on short end of each fillet, with tails over the edge. Roll up and secure each with two toothpicks. Poach the fish, turning occasionally, 10 minutes or until it turns white. Spoon some of the poaching liquid over the fish and cover the pan. Make sure you do not overcook the fish. Arrange the sole on a warm platter and sprinkle with some fresh mint.

**PREPARATION TIME:**      *20–25 minutes*

**TIME SAVER:**
Prepare the poaching mixture in advance.
Poach in the microwave on High for 5 minutes.

VARIATIONS:
- Replace the white wine with orange juice and add orange zest.
- Use fresh parsley instead of mint.

LOW-FAT OPTION:
- Replace the white wine with grape or apple juice.

# SOLE POACHED IN SPICY TOMATO-DILL SAUCE
### *Serves 2–4.*

This is a low-fat tasty dish I cooked a lot when I was losing weight. (On this episode, I was caught standing on a box at the end of the show so I could be taller than Mary Jo.)

| | |
|---|---|
| 1 tsp | vegetable oil, low in cholesterol and saturated fats |
| 2 cloves | garlic, minced |
| 1 | small onion, chopped |
| 1/2 cup | chopped fennel |
| 1/2 cup | chopped celery |
| 2 | carrots, chopped or shredded |
| 1 | sweet red pepper, chopped |
| 1 can | tomatoes (19 oz/540 mL) |
| 1 tbsp | honey OR 1/4 cup frozen apple juice concentrate, thawed |
| 1/2 tsp | finely chopped jalapeño pepper |
| 1/4 cup | chopped fresh dill |
| 1/2 cup | red wine |
| 1 | bay leaf |
| 1/2 tsp | salt |
| 1/2 tsp | black pepper |
| 4 | sole fillets |

SUGGESTED SIDE DISHES:
- Couscous with prunes
- White bean salad
- Fruit salad

In a large skillet or sauté pan, heat the oil. Sauté the garlic and onion till onion is translucent. Add the fennel, celery, carrots and red pepper. Sauté another 2–3 minutes. Add the tomatoes, honey, jalapeño pepper, dill, red wine, bay leaf, salt and pepper. Simmer on very low heat 3–5 minutes. Add the fish to the sauce and spoon the sauce over. Poach 3–5 minutes or until fish has turned white. Serve fish with sauce spooned over.

**PREPARATION TIME:** *20–25 minutes*

VARIATIONS:
- Replace the fresh dill with fresh parsley.
- Instead of sole, try snapper or grouper.
- Replace sole with chicken and cook a bit longer.

LOW-FAT OPTION:
- Leave out the oil and poach all the ingredients.

# GRILLED PEPPER-SALMON ON BED OF SLICED RED PEPPER AND GREEN ONION

*Serves 2.*

I am always impressed with how chefs create art from food. This dish is easy to present beautifully: a dollop of brilliant red pepper purée atop salmon steaks on a bed of artfully arranged sliced red pepper and green onion!

|         | Juice of 1 lemon        |
|---------|-------------------------|
| 3       | large sweet red peppers |
| 1/4 cup | apple juice             |
| 1/2 tsp | hot sauce               |
| 1/2 cup | chopped fennel          |
| 1/2 tsp | salt                    |
| 6       | green onions            |
| 2       | salmon steaks           |
| 1 tbsp  | paprika                 |
| 2 tsp   | black pepper            |

Set aside 1 tsp lemon juice. Cut one red pepper into chunks. In a food processor or in a bowl using a hand blender, purée red pepper, apple juice, hot sauce, fennel, reserved lemon juice and salt. Chill. Slice diagonally the remaining red peppers and the green onions; arrange on plates. Drizzle remaining lemon juice over salmon. Sprinkle the fish with the paprika and black pepper. Grill 3–4 minutes on each side (or sauté with some butter or oil), until salmon turns a light pink. Place grilled fish on vegetables and top with cold purée.

**PREPARATION TIME:**   *20–25 minutes*

**TIME SAVER:**
Prepare the purée in advance.

SUGGESTED SIDE DISHES:
- Scallop and mandarin orange salad on watercress
- Hummus
- Green beans with olive oil and garlic

TIP:
When grilling, make sure the heat is not too high—salmon is a delicate fish that can easily overcook.

VARIATION:
Replace salmon with boneless chicken and cook longer.

LOW-FAT OPTIONS:
Use white fish, which has less oil than salmon.
Reduce salt and replace with herbs.

# Salmon Stuffed with Wild Rice and Dill

*Serves 4–6.*

I love to cook this for friends: it is so easy. Be creative and stuff the salmon with your own version (and let me know how it turns out).

| | |
|---|---|
| 1 | whole salmon (3–5 lb) |
| 1 cup | cooked wild rice |
| 1 cup | chopped fresh dill |
| 1/2 cup | grated Parmesan cheese |
| | Juice of 1 lemon |
| 1 | medium onion, chopped |
| 2 cloves | garlic, minced |
| 1 | lemon, sliced |

**SUGGESTED SIDE DISHES:**

- Glazed baby onions
- Spinach salad with apples and walnuts
- Asparagus with yogurt and orange sauce

Remove head and tail of salmon. In a bowl, mix well the wild rice, half of the dill, Parmesan cheese, 2 tbsp of the lemon juice and onion. Arrange the garlic inside the fish, then stuff with the dill and rice mixture. Top the stuffing with the remaining dill. Place fish in a baking dish lightly coated with vegetable oil. Lay lemon slices across top of the fish. Sprinkle remaining lemon juice over and around the fish. Bake, uncovered, at 375°F for 20–25 minutes or until fish is pink and skin starts to curl. Add more lemon juice or water to the baking dish if it is dry.

**PREPARATION TIME:**     *35 minutes*

**TIME SAVER:**
Cook wild rice in the microwave 10–15 minutes, on High.

VARIATIONS:
- Replace wild rice with white rice.
- Replace the dill with finely chopped parsley.

# SALMON STEAKS WITH SAUTÉED VEGETABLES

*Serves 2.*

Although I use butter in this dish, the sauce is not cream-based, so the
fat content is lowered.

| | |
|---|---|
| 1/2 tsp | dried tarragon |
| 1/2 tsp | dried dill |
| 1/4 tsp | dried basil |
| 1/2 tsp | salt |
| 1 tsp | black pepper |
| 2 tbsp | butter |
| 1 clove | garlic, minced |
| 2 | small shallots (or 1 onion), chopped |
| 1/2 | sweet red pepper, sliced into strips |
| 1 cup | chopped mushrooms |
| 8 | asparagus stalks, chopped |
| 8 | cherry tomatoes |
| 1 | medium carrot, julienned |
| 2 | large salmon steaks |
| | Juice and zest of 1 lemon |
| 1/2 cup | white wine |

SUGGESTED SIDE DISHES:
- Poached pear salad with spinach
- Rice with black currants

*continued...*

In a small bowl, stir together the tarragon, dill, basil, salt and pepper; set aside. In a skillet, melt 1 tbsp of the butter. Sauté the garlic and shallots until translucent. Add red pepper, mushrooms, asparagus, tomatoes and carrot. Sauté 2 minutes; remove from pan and set aside. Melt the remaining butter in the skillet and gently sauté the salmon steaks 2–4 minutes on each side until light pink in color. Sprinkle half the herb mixture on the salmon. Drizzle the lemon juice over salmon. Transfer the salmon to warm plates. Add the wine to the pan along with the remaining herbs. Reduce liquid by half. Add the cooked vegetables to the skillet, stirring for 30 seconds, and arrange around the salmon. Garnish with lemon zest.

**PREPARATION TIME:** *25 minutes*

**TIME SAVER:**
Chop vegetables in a food processor.

TIP:
- When buying a whole salmon, allow about 1/3 to 1/2 lb per person.

VARIATIONS:
- Replace the salmon with swordfish.
- Replace the salmon with chicken breasts and cook longer.

LOW-FAT OPTIONS:
- Grill or poach the salmon.
- Use vegetable oil rather than butter.

# SALMON STEAKS WITH GRAPEFRUIT SAUCE

*Serves 2–4.*

During this episode, Mary Jo and I introduced two new pets: Gill and Dill, the goldfish (who were somewhat perturbed we were doing fish as the entrée). The combination of citrus and fish really works well in this recipe.

| | |
|---|---|
| 4 | salmon steaks |
| 1-1/4 cups | grapefruit juice |
| 1 | medium grapefruit, peeled and cut into small pieces (about 1 cup) |
| 2 | green onions, chopped |
| 1/4 cup | finely chopped fennel |
| 1 tsp | olive oil |
| 1/2 cup | white wine |
| 2 tbsp | chopped fresh dill |
| 1/4 tsp | grapefruit zest |
| 1/4 tsp | salt |
| 1/2 tsp | black pepper |
| 1/2 cup | low-fat sour cream or yogurt |
| 1/2 cup | table or half-and-half cream |
| | Fresh grapefruit slices for garnish |

SUGGESTED SIDE DISHES:
- Watercress and carrot salad with vinaigrette dressing
- Grilled zucchini with cold tomato sauce

*continued...*

In a shallow glass dish, marinate salmon in 1 cup of the grapefruit juice and some of the grapefruit pieces for 15 minutes, turning occasionally. In a medium saucepan over medium heat, sauté the green onions and fennel in the oil until tender. Add the wine and raise heat, cooking for 3–4 minutes to reduce liquid. Add the remaining grapefruit juice, 1/2 cup of the grapefruit pieces, the dill, zest, salt and pepper; simmer 10 minutes. Stir in the sour cream and cream; allow liquid to reduce and thicken, stirring constantly. Do not let boil or the yogurt will curdle. Keep sauce warm. Grill the salmon, brushing occasionally with the marinade, 3–4 minutes each side until the salmon turns light pink. Garnish with grapefruit slices.

**PREPARATION TIME:**     *20–25 minutes*

**TIME SAVER:**

Marinate fish the night before. Keep it covered and refrigerated until needed.

VARIATIONS:

— Replace salmon steaks with tuna, swordfish or shark.
— To serve this dish cold, omit the wine and cream and purée the sauce.

LOW-FAT OPTIONS:

— Use skim milk rather than cream; if you do, thicken the sauce with a little flour, or use more low-fat sour cream.
— Sauté the onion and fennel in some grapefruit juice instead of oil.

# TROUT STUFFED WITH DILL AND LEMON RICE

*Serves 2–4.*

This trout has a very fresh and light flavor. This was a recipe that my father would make and impress the whole family with. (He would put the trout, in foil, on the barbecue.)

| | |
|---|---|
| 2 | whole trout |
| 1/4 cup | lemon juice |
| 1 cup | cooked rice |
| 1/2 cup | finely chopped fresh dill |
| 1/4 cup | chopped fresh chives |
| 1 tsp | lemon zest |
| 1/2 tsp | coriander seeds |
| 1 tbsp | vegetable or olive oil |
| 1/4 tsp | salt |
| 1/2 tsp | black pepper |
| 12 slices | lemon |

SUGGESTED SIDE DISHES:
- Stir-fried vegetables
- Asparagus with Parmesan cheese and butter
- Bruschetta (recipe on p. 2)

If you prefer, remove heads and tails from the trout; lay trout on a sheet of foil. Set aside 1 tbsp of the lemon juice. In a bowl, mix together the rice, dill, remaining lemon juice, chives, lemon zest, coriander seeds, oil, salt and pepper. Stuff trout with the rice mixture. Place two lemon slices inside each fish and arrange four more on the top. Drizzle reserved lemon juice over the fish. Wrap tightly in foil and bake at 350°F for 10–15 minutes. Trout is done when it starts to separate.

**PREPARATION TIME:**    *25 minutes*

TIP:
- Calculate cooking time by measuring the fish at its thickest point and allowing 8–10 minutes per inch of thickness.

VARIATIONS:
- Add 1/4 cup chopped fresh coriander to the stuffing.
- Replace the trout with salmon or red snapper and adjust cooking time according to the tip.
- Replace lemon juice, slices and zest with orange.

LOW-FAT OPTION:
- Replace the oil with 2 tbsp of vegetable stock.

# TUNA STEAKS WITH GINGER AND ORANGE

*Serves 2–4.*

Tuna steak, which is very rich, is best grilled. In winter, use an indoor grill.

| | |
|---|---|
| 1 | seedless orange |
| 1/4 cup | light soy sauce |
| 1 clove | garlic, minced |
| 1 tsp | chopped fresh ginger (or 1/2 tsp dried) |
| 1/2 cup | orange juice |
| 1 tbsp | lemon juice |
| 2 | tuna steaks |
| 1/4 cup | finely chopped chives for garnish |

**SUGGESTED SIDE DISHES:**
- Brussels sprouts and almonds
- Wok-fried Oriental noodles

Remove 1 tbsp zest from the orange; set aside. Cut 6 thin slices from orange; set aside. In a shallow glass baking dish, combine the soy sauce, garlic, ginger, orange juice, lemon juice and the reserved zest. Marinate tuna steaks for 15 minutes, turning often. Grill tuna 4–5 minutes on each side depending on thickness, basting frequently with the marinade. Tuna is done when it starts to turn a lighter color. Meanwhile, grill the orange slices on each side. Garnish tuna with orange slices and chives.

**PREPARATION TIME:**    *25–30 minutes*

**TIME SAVER:**

Begin marinating the tuna in the morning or even the night before. Keep it covered and refrigerated and it will be ready to grill when you come home.

VARIATIONS:
- Replace tuna with swordfish.
- Replace fresh ginger with 1/4 cup finely chopped fennel.

LOW-FAT OPTION:
- This is already a great low-fat recipe.

# Fish Kebob

*Serves 4–6.*

If you don't have a barbecue or indoor grill, just use the broiler in your oven. I especially like this fish kebob variation because it has a very meaty texture but is very low in fat.

| | |
|---|---|
| 1/2 cup | chopped fresh dill |
| 1/2 cup | lemon juice |
| 3 cloves | garlic, mashed |
| 1 tsp | paprika |
| 1 tsp | sugar, or equivalent liquid sweetener OR 1/4 cup frozen apple juice concentrate, thawed |
| 1/2 tsp | salt |
| 1/2 tsp | black pepper |
| 1 | large tuna steak, cut into 1-1/2–2-inch pieces |
| 1 | large swordfish steak, cut into 1-1/2–2-inch pieces |
| 1 | sweet red pepper, cut into 1-1/2–2-inch pieces |
| 2 | medium onions, cut into 1-1/2–2-inch pieces |

SUGGESTED SIDE DISHES:
- Baked or grilled vegetables
- Baked herbed mushrooms
- Couscous with chopped dates

Soak four to six 8-inch wooden skewers. In a shallow glass baking dish, combine the dill, lemon juice, garlic, paprika, sugar, salt and pepper. Marinate fish pieces 15 minutes. Alternately thread fish, red pepper and onion onto skewers. Grill, occasionally brushing with marinade and turning, 8–10 minutes, until the meat starts to lighten in color.

**PREPARATION TIME:**     *25–30 minutes*

**TIME SAVER:**
Marinate the fish in the morning or even the night before and let it sit, covered, in the fridge all day. Doing this will make it even more flavorful.

VARIATIONS:
- Replace tuna or swordfish with salmon.
- Replace the seafood with chicken pieces and veal pieces; increase the cooking time.

# Swordfish with Pepper, Green Onions and White Wine

*Serves 2.*

Swordfish is one of my favorites because of its meaty texture. It's also extremely nutritious.

| | |
|---|---|
| 2 | swordfish steaks |
| 1 tbsp | cracked black pepper |
| 1/2 tsp | salt |
| 1 tbsp | olive oil |
| 2 | shallots, chopped |
| 1/4 cup | finely chopped fennel, (optional) |
| 8 | green onions, cut into large pieces |
| 1/2 cup | white wine |
| 1/4 cup | low-fat yogurt |
| 1 tbsp | all-purpose flour |

SUGGESTED SIDE DISHES:
- Pasta salad
- Steamed brussels sprouts with lemon juice
- Flatbread with sliced red onion, rosemary and olive oil

Arrange swordfish in a nonstick baking dish and sprinkle both sides evenly with pepper and salt. Set aside. In a small skillet, heat the olive oil. Sauté the shallots, fennel (if using), and half of the green onions about 2 minutes or until shallots are soft. Reduce heat and stir in wine, yogurt and flour. Simmer, stirring gently to prevent curdling, about 2 minutes until thickened. Pour sauce over swordfish and bake, uncovered, at 375°F for 10–12 minutes until swordfish turns white. Place remaining green onions on plates and arrange fish and sauce on top.

**PREPARATION TIME:** *20 minutes*

**TIME SAVER:**
Wrap seasoned fish in foil and bake while preparing the sauce.

VARIATIONS:
- Replace the shallots with a small cooking onion.
- Replace swordfish with tuna, trout or even chicken. (Increase the cooking time if you use chicken.)

# ROASTED JUMBO SHRIMP WITH SPINACH AND RICE

*Serves 4–6.*

This dish was part of our "Roasting Show," a theme requested by our viewers. Poultry, meat and seafood were all featured. Not only is this recipe quick and easy, but it is also low in fat.

| | |
|---|---|
| 1 cup | basmati rice |
| 1/2 cup | chopped fennel |
| 2 cloves | garlic, minced |
| 1/4 cup | light soy sauce |
| 1 tsp | chopped fresh ginger |
| Pinch | saffron |
| 2 cups | boiling fish stock or apple juice |
| 12 | medium to large jumbo shrimp, peeled and deveined |
| 2 cups | shredded fresh spinach |

SUGGESTED SIDE DISHES:
- Tossed leaf lettuce salad with Dijon vinaigrette
- Bruschetta topped with chopped zucchini, garlic, olive oil and basil

In a large casserole dish, combine the rice, fennel, garlic, soy sauce, ginger and saffron. Stir in the boiling stock. Bake, covered, at 350°F for 10 minutes. Stir in the shrimp and spinach. Bake, uncovered, another 10 minutes or until rice is done.

**PREPARATION TIME:** *25–35 minutes*

**TIME SAVER:**
Microwave fish stock or apple juice for 3–4 minutes on High while you are preparing other ingredients.

VARIATIONS:
- Replace the rice with couscous, diced potatoes or polenta.
- Replace the shrimp with other seafood such as swordfish, tuna, scallops, crab or lobster. Or use any combination of these.

# SCALLOPS WITH LEMON-ORANGE SAUCE
*Serves 4–6.*

Most people don't realize how much flavor comes from only a small amount of orange or lemon zest: be careful and experiment. After this show, one viewer wrote to say how much she loved our recipes because most consisted of easily available food "dressed up for a dinner party."

| | |
|---|---|
| 1 | small onion, chopped |
| 1 tbsp | olive oil |
| 2 lb | large bay scallops (about 2 cups) |
| 2 tbsp | combined orange and lemon zest |
| 1/2 tsp | black pepper |
| 1/4 cup | orange juice |
| 2 tbsp | lemon juice |
| 3/4 cup | low-fat yogurt or sour cream |
| 1 tsp | dried tarragon |
| 1/4 tsp | salt |
| | Orange slices for garnish |

SUGGESTED SIDE DISHES:
- Spinach soup with coconut milk
- Pita bread with fresh herbs

In a large skillet, sauté the onion in oil for 2 minutes or until soft. Add the scallops, 1 tbsp of the zest and the pepper. Sauté 1–2 minutes. If scallops are small, remove and set aside. Add the orange juice and lemon juice; simmer half a minute. Reduce heat and stir in yogurt, tarragon, remaining zest and the salt; simmer, stirring gently, 5 minutes or until the sauce thickens. Add reserved small scallops to the sauce and heat through. Serve over egg noodles and garnish with remaining zest and orange slices.

VARIATIONS:
- Instead of scallops, use jumbo shrimp or clams.
- Replace yogurt with table cream to enrich the sauce.

LOW-FAT OPTION:
- Replace the oil with 2 tbsp of orange juice.

**PREPARATION TIME:**        *20 minutes*

# SHRIMP AND SCALLOP GINGER STIR-FRY

*Serves 4–6.*

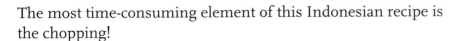

The most time-consuming element of this Indonesian recipe is the chopping!

| | |
|---|---|
| 1/2 cup | chopped green onions |
| 2 cloves | garlic, minced |
| 1 tbsp | olive oil |
| 1 tbsp | sesame oil |
| 1 tbsp | chopped fresh ginger |
| 10 | large jumbo shrimp, peeled and deveined |
| 1 cup | medium-large scallops |
| 1 cup | chopped mushrooms |
| 1 | sweet red pepper, sliced |
| 1 | sweet green pepper, sliced |
| 1/2 cup | sliced purple cabbage |
| 2 | celery stalks, sliced diagonally |
| 2 | large carrots, sliced lengthwise and cut in half |
| 1 tsp | dried oregano |
| 1 cup | bean sprouts |
| 1/2 cup | chopped fresh spinach |
| 1/4 cup | soy or tamari sauce |
| 2 tbsp | honey |
| 1/2 tsp | salt |
| 1/2 tsp | black pepper |
| 1 tsp | sesame seeds |
| 1 tbsp | crushed almonds |

SUGGESTED SIDE DISHES:
- Mushroom fried rice
- Vegetables rolled up in pita

*continued...*

In a wok or large skillet, stir-fry the green onions and garlic in olive and sesame oils until tender or translucent. Add the ginger and stir-fry until white or tender. Add the shrimp and scallops; stir-fry 2–3 minutes until the shrimp turn pink and the scallops turn white. Remove and set aside. Add the mushrooms, red and green peppers, cabbage, celery, carrots and oregano; stir-fry until vegetables are tender, about 2 minutes. Add the bean sprouts and spinach; stir-fry 1 minute. Make a well in the center and add soy sauce and honey. Stir-fry 1 minute. Add the seafood, salt and pepper; toss well. Serve sprinkled with sesame seeds and almonds.

**PREPARATION TIME:**     *20–25 minutes*

**TIME SAVER:**
Have your family or friends help with the chopping.

VARIATIONS:
— Replace the seafood with chicken or tofu.
— Add fresh fruits such as pears, apples, peaches or oranges.

LOW-FAT OPTION:
— Use canola oil rather than olive and sesame oils.

# ZESTY MUSSELS IN RED WINE WITH VEGETABLES
*Serves 4–6.*

This is a quick dinner over pasta or rice. I sometimes serve it as an appetizer with a hearty bread so you can dip into the sauce.

| | |
|---|---|
| 1 tbsp | olive oil |
| 1 | onion (or 2 shallots), chopped |
| 2 cloves | garlic, coarsely chopped |
| 2 | large carrots, julienned |
| 4 | celery stalks, sliced diagonally |
| 1 cup | chopped zucchini |
| 1 cup | chopped mushrooms |
| 1/2 cup | chopped fennel |
| 1 can | stewed tomatoes (19 oz/540 mL) |
| 1/2 cup | red wine |
| 1/2 tsp | finely chopped hot peppers |
| 1 tsp | dried tarragon |
| 1/2 tsp | dried basil |
| 1/2 tsp | salt |
| 1 tsp | black pepper |
| 4 dozen | mussels, cleaned |

SUGGESTED SIDE DISHES:
- Tofu baked with soy sauce and garlic
- Salad with oranges and citrus dressing

In a large saucepan or crock pot, heat the oil. Sauté the onion, garlic, carrots, celery, zucchini, mushrooms and fennel 2–3 minutes until tender. Add the tomatoes, red wine, hot peppers, tarragon, basil, salt and pepper. Bring to a boil. Reduce heat and simmer 10–15 minutes. Add the mussels. Cook, covered, 2–3 minutes or until the mussels open. Discard any mussels that do not open. Serve over pasta.

**PREPARATION TIME:**     *20–25 minutes*

VARIATION:
— Replace mussels with fresh clams.

LOW-FAT OPTION:
— Replace the red wine with grape juice.

# HERBED CRAB CAKES

*Serves 2–4.*

These crab cakes are surprisingly easy to prepare: I serve these as a main dish for brunch or as an appetizer with dinner.

| | |
|---|---|
| 1 lb | fresh crab meat |
| 1/4 cup | dry bread crumbs |
| 2 | celery stalks, finely chopped |
| 1/2 cup | chopped sweet red pepper |
| 1 tsp | chopped fresh tarragon |
| 1 tsp | chopped fresh dill |
| 1 tsp | chopped fresh basil |
| 1 tsp | chopped fresh oregano |
| 1/2 tsp | paprika |
| 1/2 tsp | salt |
| 1/2 tsp | black pepper |
| 1/2 tsp | finely chopped jalapeño pepper |
| 1/4 cup | low-fat yogurt |

### DIP:

| | |
|---|---|
| 1 cup | low-fat yogurt |
| 1/4 cup | chopped fresh dill |
| 2 tbsp | chopped chives |
| 1/2 tsp | salt |
| 1/2 tsp | black pepper |

SUGGESTED SIDE DISHES:

- Spinach salad with pine nuts and apples
- Baked potatoes
- Deep-fried artichokes

In a bowl, combine crab meat, bread crumbs, celery, red pepper, tarragon, dill, basil, oregano, paprika, salt, pepper, jalapeño pepper and yogurt. Mix well and shape into four crab cakes. Arrange crab cakes in a nonstick baking dish and broil 4–5 minutes on each side or until crispy and golden. Serve with the low-fat dip.

# HERBED CRAB CAKES

*continued*

**DIP:**

In a small bowl, stir together yogurt, dill, chives, salt and pepper.

**PREPARATION TIME:** *20 minutes*

**TIME SAVER:**

Process all the crab cake ingredients together in a food processor.

VARIATION:

—— Replace the crab meat with fresh or canned tuna or salmon.

LOW-FAT OPTION:

—— Replace bread crumbs with ground-up low-sodium rice cakes.

# SQUID IN SPICY TOMATO SAUCE

*Serves 2–4.*

This recipe is one of the simplest to prepare. I serve it as a main course over pasta or as a cold dish for lunch. Be warned! It is hot, so adjust the hot sauce or hot pepper content to taste.

| | |
|---|---|
| 2 tbsp | vegetable oil |
| 4 | large squid, sliced into rings about 1/2-inch thick (about 3 cups) |
| 1 cup | chopped onions or shallots |
| 1/2 cup | chopped celery |
| 1/2 cup | chopped sweet red pepper |
| 1/2 cup | chopped fennel |
| 1/2 cup | chopped fresh basil |
| 1/2 cup | chopped fresh dill |
| 1/2 tsp | salt |
| 1 tsp | black pepper |
| 1 can | tomatoes (19 oz/540 mL) |
| 1 tbsp | hot sauce OR |
| | 1 tsp finely choppedhot pepper |

In a large lidded skillet, heat the oil over medium heat. Gently sauté the squid 3 minutes or until rings turn white. Add the onions, celery, red peppers and fennel; sauté, stirring, another 3–4 minutes. Reduce heat to low and add the basil, dill, salt and pepper. Simmer 2–3 minutes. Add the tomatoes and hot sauce; simmer, covered, another 15 minutes. Serve over pasta or rice.

**PREPARATION TIME:** *25 minutes*

SUGGESTED SIDE DISH:
• Couscous with raisins

TIP:
➤— Don't worry about the squid ending up chewy or tough, as the sautéing and the simmering in the sauce make the squid tender.

VARIATIONS:
— For a vegetarian meal, replace squid with mushrooms. Keep in mind that mushrooms shrink, so you will require 3–4 cups of chopped or sliced mushrooms.
— Add other types of seafood, if desired.
— For meat lovers, replace the squid with chicken or Italian sausage.
— Replace the fennel with 1/2 cup more celery.

LOW-FAT OPTION:
— Leave out the oil and sauté the squid in a nonstick skillet.

# STUFFED CALAMARI WITH ZESTY TOMATO SAUCE

*Serves 4–6.*

This calamari is an unusual combination of seafood with turkey, rice and cheese in a tomato sauce. Although easy to prepare, it can also be a bit messy. Just be organized in the kitchen and it will all come together. On this episode, Mary Jo was much entertained by my squid-stuffing style.

| | |
|---|---|
| 1-1/2 cups | cooked rice |
| 1/2 cup | chopped fennel |
| 1/2 | sweet red pepper, chopped |
| 4 | fresh or frozen squid tentacles, cleaned |
| 4 slices | smoked turkey breast |
| 4 slices | Swiss cheese |
| 1 | small onion, chopped |
| 3 cloves | garlic, minced |
| 1/2 | sweet green pepper, chopped |
| 1 can | crushed tomatoes (19 oz/540 mL) |
| 1 tsp | dried basil |
| 1 tsp | hot sauce (or more to taste) |

SUGGESTED SIDE DISHES:
- Potato and leek soup
- Steamed mussels
- No-Mayo, No-Oil Caesar Salad (recipe on p. 20)

In a bowl, mix together the rice, fennel and red pepper. Line the inside of the squid with the slices of turkey and cheese. Stuff the squid with the rice mixture. Transfer squid to a baking dish just large enough to hold them; set aside. In a nonstick skillet, sauté the onions, garlic and green pepper until translucent. Stir in the tomatoes, basil and hot sauce. Spoon the sauce over the squid and bake, covered, at 350°F for 20–25 minutes until squid is tender.

**PREPARATION TIME:** *30–35 minutes*

VARIATIONS:
— Replace Swiss cheese with cheddar.
— Instead of canned tomatoes, use 4 fresh tomatoes, puréed with 1 cup of water and 1 tsp of tomato paste.

LOW-FAT OPTION:
— Use a low-fat or skim-milk Swiss cheese.

It gives me great pleasure to watch the two of you making those delicious dishes of low *Calorie* and low *Fat* foods. I rush to my TV set every evening to see what the two of you are making so I will know *What's for Dinner* around here.

I really enjoyed watching you whip up that turkey sausage with spicy tomato sauce, stir-fried noodles and vegetables, baked couscous with chopped spinach and fennel, turkey shepherd's pie and especially that spicy seafood paella dish, which I would love to have the recipe for...

I do enjoy watching both of you [having fun] in the kithen instead of just slaving over a hot stove and hoping to heaven the outcome will be something you can enjoy or eat after cooking it. I cook for six people in this household so you can imagine what creativity I have to have ... to fix dinner every night.

Do keep up the good cooking! When I see you start to cook, I can almost smell it. It always looks so tasty.


Sincerly,


*Ann*
Westbank, B.C.

# MEATLESS MAIN DISHES

Being a vegetarian, it's always great to find healthy, tasty new recipes. The meal that was prepared on *What's for Dinner?* (Thai Noodles) certainly looked great.

I could almost smell everything cooking…

Thank you,

*Roxanne*
Welland, Ont.

# RATATOUILLE

*Serves 4–6.*

This recipe is great as a vegetarian main dish with rice. Or serve it the next day as a side dish, or mixed with eggs to create a vegetarian omelette. (During this episode, I tried to find a husband on air for my sister Diane.)

| | |
|---|---|
| 2 tbsp | olive oil |
| 3 | large onions, chopped |
| 3 cloves | garlic, minced |
| 2 | large zucchini, chopped |
| 2 | sweet green peppers, chopped |
| 1 | sweet red pepper, chopped |
| 2 cups | chopped eggplant |
| 1 can | stewed tomatoes (28 oz/796 mL) |
| 1 tbsp | sugar or equivalent sweetener |
| 1/2 tsp | dried basil |
| 1/2 tsp | dried thyme |
| 1/2 tsp | salt |
| 1/2 tsp | black pepper |

SUGGESTED SIDE DISHES:
- Lentils with pearl onions and shaved carrot
- No-Mayo, No-Oil Caesar Salad (recipe on p. 20)

In a crock pot or large heavy saucepan, heat the oil and sauté the onions and garlic until onions are translucent. Do not burn the garlic. Add the zucchini, green and red peppers, eggplant, tomatoes, sugar, basil, thyme, salt and pepper. Reduce heat to low and cook, stirring occasionally, 20 minutes or until vegetables are tender but not mushy. If too much liquid evaporates, just add some tomato juice or water mixed with tomato paste. Serve hot or cold, over pasta or rice.

**PREPARATION TIME:**      *30 minutes*

LOW-FAT OPTIONS:
— Instead of sautéing in oil, use vegetable stock.
— Use apple juice concentrate instead of sugar.

# GRILLED MUSHROOMS AND VEGETABLES COATED WITH HERBS

*Serves 8.*

I have many friends who are vegetarian. I prepare this low-fat dish for them in summer, and they love it.

| | |
|---|---|
| 2 | red peppers |
| 2 | zucchini |
| 1 bunch | broccoli |
| 1/2 head | cauliflower |
| 1 | red onion |
| 25–30 | large assorted mushrooms |
| 1/2 | fennel bulb, chopped into 1-inch pieces |
| 1 tbsp | olive oil |
| 1 cup | chopped fresh parsley |
| 1/2 cup | chopped fresh dill |
| 1/4 cup | chopped fresh rosemary |
| 1/4 cup | chopped fresh oregano |
| 1/4 cup | chopped fresh coriander |
| 1/2 tsp | salt |
| 1/2 tsp | black pepper |
| 1/2 cup | lemon juice |

SUGGESTED SIDE DISHES:
- Red pepper and corn relish
- Pita bread with chick peas, tomato and basil
- Rice with pineapple juice and pieces

Soak eight 8-inch wooden skewers. Chop into large pieces the red peppers, zucchini, broccoli, cauliflower, onion, mushrooms and fennel. Place vegetables and oil in a large bowl. Add parsley, dill, rosemary, oregano, coriander, salt, pepper and lemon juice. Toss to coat well. Thread vegetables onto skewers and grill 5–10 minutes.

**PREPARATION TIME:**     *25 minutes*

**TIME SAVER:**
Get some help with the chopping from your friends or family. This is a great "social recipe" that everyone can assist with.

VARIATION:
⬤— Use dried herbs.

# VEGETABLE CURRY MEDLEY
*Serves 2–4.*

This vegetable dish combines several exotic flavors. If you wish, leave out the coconut milk to reduce the fat content.

| | |
|---|---|
| 2 tbsp | vegetable oil |
| 1 cup | chopped red onion |
| 4 cloves | garlic, chopped |
| 3 tbsp | mild curry paste |
| 1 cup | unsweetened coconut milk |
| 1/2 cup | chopped fresh coriander |
| 1/2 tsp | hot sauce |
| 1/2 tsp | salt |
| 1/4 cup | water |
| 1/2 | cauliflower, chopped |
| 1 cup | chopped broccoli |
| 1 cup | snow peas |
| 1 cup | carrots, sliced thinly |
| 1 cup | canned chick peas, drained and rinsed |
| 1/2 cup | yogurt |

**SUGGESTED SIDE DISHES:**
- Brown rice with raisins
- Pita bread with olive oil and goat cheese

In a wok or large lidded skillet, heat the oil and gently sauté the onions 2 minutes. Add the garlic and sauté another 2 minutes. Add the curry paste, coconut milk, coriander, hot sauce, salt and water. Reduce heat to low and simmer 5 minutes. Add the cauliflower, broccoli, snow peas, carrots and chick peas. Cover and simmer, stirring occasionally, 4–5 minutes. Do not overcook the vegetables. Stir in the yogurt and cook another minute.

**PREPARATION TIME:**     *15–20 minutes*

**TIME SAVER:**
Microwave the cauliflower, broccoli and carrots at High for 2 minutes.

VARIATIONS:
- Add firm tofu or sliced chicken breast.
- Replace the fresh coriander with 1 tsp ground coriander or 1/2 cup chopped parsley.
- Instead of curry paste, use 1/2 tsp fresh sliced ginger.

LOW-FAT OPTION:
- Use low-fat or non-fat yogurt or sour cream.

# STIR-FRIED NOODLES AND VEGETABLES

*Serves 4–6.*

I cook for a lot of people with different food requirements. This meatless meal is a favorite of both my vegetarian and non-vegetarian friends. Try this recipe on your family and friends.

| | |
|---|---|
| 1 tsp | sesame oil |
| 1 | small onion, sliced |
| 1 | sweet green pepper, chopped |
| 1 | sweet red pepper, chopped |
| 1 cup | chopped broccoli |
| 1/2 cup | bean sprouts |
| 1/2 cup | snow peas, halved |
| 1 tsp | chopped fresh ginger |
| 2 tbsp | light soy sauce |
| 2 cups | cooked spaghetti or egg noodles |
| 2 tsp | all-purpose flour or rice flour |
| 1/4 cup | apple juice |
| 1 cup | fresh or frozen peas |

SUGGESTED SIDE DISHES:
- Baked tofu with garlic
- Black bean soup
- Mixed green salad

In a wok or large skillet, heat the oil. Add the onion, green and red peppers, broccoli, sprouts and snow peas. Stir-fry 2 minutes or until vegetables are tender but not overdone. Stir in ginger, soy sauce and spaghetti; stir-fry 3–4 minutes. Whisk the flour into the apple juice. Make a hole in the center of the wok; pour in juice and add peas, stirring until the liquid thickens, about 1–2 minutes. Toss everything well to combine.

**PREPARATION TIME:** *15–20 minutes*

**TIME SAVER:**
Chop the vegetables in a food processor.

VARIATION:
Replace spaghetti or egg noodles with rice noodles.

LOW-FAT OPTION:
Replace the sesame oil with canola or vegetable oil.

# SPICY THAI NOODLES WITH TOFU

*Serves 4.*

This is another recipe that allows you to use additional or substitute ingredients you already have in the kitchen. The kids will love the flavor of this meal, and the added value is that it's bursting with nutrition.

| | |
|---|---|
| 2 tbsp | olive oil |
| 1 lb | firm tofu, sliced |
| 3 cloves | garlic, minced |
| 1/2 tsp | minced fresh ginger |
| 1 cup | sliced shiitake mushrooms |
| 1/4 cup | soy sauce |
| 1 tbsp | vegetable stock |
| 1 tbsp | peanut butter |
| 1 tsp | finely chopped jalapeño pepper |
| 2 cups | cooked rice noodles |
| 1 | sweet red pepper, chopped |
| 1 cup | cooked spinach |

**SUGGESTED SIDE DISHES:**
- Grilled red, green and orange peppers
- Rice with curry and banana

In a wok or large skillet, heat the oil. Stir-fry the tofu, garlic, ginger and mushrooms until tender. Remove tofu and set aside. Add soy sauce, vegetable stock, and then peanut butter and jalapeño pepper. Mix together. Add noodles, red pepper and spinach. Stir-fry 3–4 minutes or till liquid is reduced by half. Return tofu to wok and mix well.

**PREPARATION TIME:**     *20–25 minutes*

**TIME SAVER:**
Chop vegetables in a food processor.

VARIATION:
— Replace rice noodles with spaghetti or angel hair pasta.

LOW-FAT OPTIONS:
— Use low-sodium soy sauce.
— Replace oil with vegetable stock.
— Use calorie-reduced tofu.

# Tofu Stir-Fry with Mandarin Oranges

*Serves 2–4.*

This stir-fry has long been one of my favorite vegetarian dishes. Tofu (a chameleon of vegetables) assumes the flavor of whatever spices, herbs and vegetables are used in a dish. (It's also an excellent source of vegetable protein.) Even if you think you don't like tofu, this is one tofu dish you really must try.

| | |
|---|---|
| 2 tsp | olive oil |
| 1 pkg | firm tofu, cubed (1 lb) |
| 1 | red onion, sliced |
| 1 | sweet red pepper, sliced in strips |
| 1 | sweet green pepper, sliced in strips |
| 2 | medium carrots, sliced |
| 1 cup | chopped broccoli |
| 1/2 tsp | chopped fresh ginger (or 1/4 tsp ground) |
| 1 cup | bean sprouts |
| 1/4 cup | orange juice |
| 1 cup | canned mandarin oranges, drained |
| 1/4 tsp | salt |
| 1/2 tsp | black pepper |
| 1 tbsp | orange zest for garnish |

**SUGGESTED SIDE DISHES:**
- Chick peas and basmati rice with spinach
- Shredded carrot and radish salad

**TIPS:**
- Firm tofu is slightly higher in vitamins and most minerals than regular tofu.
- The high heat of the wok and the oil seals in juices, preserves color and flavor.

**VARIATIONS:**
- Instead of red peppers, use sweet yellow peppers.
- Use apple juice instead of orange juice.
- Replace tofu with sliced chicken breast.

**LOW-FAT OPTION:**
- Cook vegetables in orange juice instead of oil.

In a wok or large skillet, heat the oil over high heat. Stir-fry the tofu until slightly golden at edges. Remove the tofu and set aside. Stir-fry the onion, red and green peppers, carrots, broccoli and ginger 5 minutes. Add the bean sprouts and stir-fry 1–2 minutes. Reduce heat to medium and stir in tofu, orange juice, salt and pepper; cook about 2 minutes. Stir in the mandarin oranges and cook for 1 minute. Arrange on plates and garnish with orange zest.

**PREPARATION TIME:**     *20 minutes*

# VEGETABLE AND TOFU BROCHETTES

*Serves 6–8.*

At home, I like to prepare several variations of brochettes. You can prepare these healthy low-fat brochettes any time, as your local super-market should have the ingredients all year long. (I pulled out the telephone book, yet again, for this episode so I could be taller than Mary Jo. It's incredible how one telephone book can bring so much pleasure.)

| | |
|---|---|
| 2 cloves | garlic, minced |
| 1 tsp | dried basil |
| 1 tsp | dried oregano |
| 1 tsp | dried tarragon |
| 1/2 tsp | salt |
| 1/2 tsp | black pepper |
| 1/2 cup | light soy or tamari sauce |
| 1 tsp | olive oil |
| 1 lb | firm tofu, cubed |
| 2 | sweet red or green peppers, cut into large squares |
| 1 | large zucchini, sliced |
| 2 cups | sliced large assorted mushrooms |
| 1 cup | cubed eggplant |
| 1 cup | chopped fennel |
| 1 | medium red onion, cut in chunks |

SUGGESTED SIDE DISHES:
- Lentil-onion salad
- Cold peach-apricot soup

Soak eight 8-inch wooden skewers. In a large bowl, mix well the garlic, basil, oregano, tarragon, salt, pepper, soy sauce and oil. Add tofu, red pepper, zucchini, mush-rooms, eggplant and fennel. Toss to coat well. Thread onion chunks and other vegetables onto skewers. Grill till marks are present, 5–8 minutes.

**PREPARATION TIME:**   *20–25 minutes*

**TIME SAVER:**

Prepare vegetables (except the onion) and tofu and toss them with herb-soy sauce mixture in the morning or even the night before. This serves two purposes: marinating all day will make the flavor better, and it won't take you so long to get dinner on the table.

VARIATION:
Replace the tofu with firm fish or chicken pieces.

# VEGETABLE CASSEROLE WITH TOMATO AND TOFU

*Serves 4–6.*

I created this dish for my vegetarian friend Vicki when I wanted to prepare a dinner that was flavorful and interesting. She has since served it at every dinner party!

| | |
|---|---|
| 4 | carrots, sliced diagonally |
| 4 | celery stalks, cut in chunks |
| 4 | medium potatoes, cubed |
| 4 | large tomatoes, cubed |
| 1 | medium red onion, cubed |
| 1 | sweet green pepper, cubed |
| 1 cup | cubed eggplant |
| 1 cup | cubed butternut squash |
| 1 lb | firm tofu, cubed |
| 1 can | crushed tomatoes (19 oz/540 mL) |
| 1 | sweet red pepper, quartered |
| 4 cloves | garlic, halved |
| 1/2 cup | soft tofu |
| 1/4 cup | frozen apple juice concentrate, thawed |
| 1/4 cup | vegetable stock |
| 1 tsp | dried basil |
| 1 tsp | dried oregano |
| 1/2 tsp | dried sage |
| 1/2 tsp | salt |
| 1/2 tsp | black pepper |
| 1 | bay leaf |

SUGGESTED SIDE DISHES:
- Spinach salad with optional bacon
- Rice cooked with apples and apple juice

In a large casserole dish, combine the carrots, celery, potatoes, fresh tomatoes, onion, green pepper, eggplant, squash, firm tofu and canned tomatoes. In a blender or food processor, purée until smooth the red pepper, garlic, soft tofu, apple juice concentrate, vegetable stock, basil, oregano, sage, salt and pepper. Pour the sauce over the vegetables, add the bay leaf, and bake, uncovered, at 350°F for 15–20 minutes, checking the vegetables occasionally. When vegetables are tender, discard the bay leaf and serve.

**PREPARATION TIME:**     *25–30 minutes*

VARIATIONS:
- Add seafood, if desired.
- Sprinkle grated Parmesan cheese on the top 5 minutes before done and allow it to get golden brown.

# Eggplant Casserole with Herb Tofu or Cheddar Cheese

*Serves 4–6.*

This casserole is a good one-pot meal. Most of the time spent on this recipe is with your knife, chopping. If you use tofu, this is a low-fat, guilt-free meal.

| | |
|---|---|
| 1 can | crushed tomatoes (28 oz/796 mL) |
| 1 tbsp | tomato paste |
| 2 cloves | garlic, halved |
| 1/2 cup | fresh parsley (or 1 tbsp dried) |
| 1/2 cup | fresh oregano (or 1 tsp dried) |
| 1/2 tsp | salt |
| 1/2 tsp | black pepper |
| 1 cup | mashed soft herb tofu or shredded cheddar cheese |
| 1 | large eggplant, thinly sliced crosswise |
| 1 | medium onion, thinly sliced |
| 1 cup | sliced mushrooms |
| 2 cups | thinly sliced broccoli |
| 1 | sweet red pepper, chopped |
| 1 | sweet green pepper, chopped |
| 1 cup | snow peas |

In a food processor, combine tomatoes, tomato paste, garlic, parsley, oregano, salt, pepper and herb tofu (if using). Purée and set aside. In a 13- x 9-inch lasagna dish, layer eggplant. Top with some of the onion, mushrooms, broccoli, red and green peppers and snow peas. Spoon some of the tomato sauce over the vegetables and sprinkle with cheese (if using). Repeat with remaining eggplant, vegetables and sauce, finishing with cheese on top. Bake, uncovered, at 375°F for 20 minutes or until vegetables are tender and slightly browned.

**PREPARATION TIME:** *30–35 minutes*

SUGGESTED SIDE DISH:
- Rice cooked with dates and apple juice

TIP:
- Broccoli is a good source of vitamin C and fiber, not to mention low in calories.

VARIATION:
- Purée 4 fresh tomatoes, 1/2 cup water and 1 tsp tomato paste instead of the canned tomatoes.

LOW-FAT OPTION:
- For lower-calorie or -fat content, use the tofu instead of the cheese.

# TOFU BURGERS

*Serves 4–6.*

These burgers were prepared on the "Kids' Show." Jake, whom we were babysitting that day, really enjoyed getting his hands into the mixture to make the patties.

| | |
|---|---|
| 2 cups | canned chick peas |
| 1 lb | soft tofu |
| 1 cup | dry bread crumbs |
| 1/2 cup | chopped green onions |
| 1 clove | garlic, chopped |
| 1 tbsp | paprika |
| 1 tbsp | honey |
| 1 | egg |
| 1 tsp | vegetable or soy oil |

In a food processor, purée chick peas. Add tofu, bread crumbs, green onions, garlic, paprika, honey and egg and mix well. Make patties about 4 inches across and 1 inch thick. Pan fry in oil on medium heat for 2–3 minutes on each side or until golden brown. Serve with an assortment of buns, condiments and toppings.

**PREPARATION TIME:** *30 minutes*

VARIATION:

— For slightly different traditional burgers, replace the tofu with lean ground meat.

# ROASTED POTATOES AND SWEET POTATOES WITH MARSHMALLOWS AND BROWN SUGAR

*Serves 4 as a side dish.*

This dish was also prepared on the "Kids' Show," which brought positive viewer responses from children across the country.
(Jake did think I was taller than Mary Jo. I am!)

| | |
|---|---|
| 3 | medium baking potatoes |
| 1 | sweet potato |
| 1/2 cup | apple juice |
| 1 tbsp | brown sugar |
| 1/2 tsp | cinnamon |
| 1 cup | small marshmallows |

Chop potatoes and sweet potato and microwave, covered, at High for 2–3 minutes. Transfer to a small baking dish, pour apple juice over, and roast at 400°F for 20 minutes. Sprinkle with brown sugar and cinnamon. When potatoes are tender, top with marshmallows and broil till golden. Watch carefully, as the marshmallows burn easily.

**PREPARATION TIME:**     *30 minutes*

**TIME SAVER:**
Get as many children as you can find to help you.

# BREADS, PITA AND PIZZA

I really enjoy watching your show. My seven-month-old daughter starts laughing and rolling and jiggling around when she hears the theme music to *What's for Dinner?*

It's great to see you two working so well in the kitchen and getting it all done—in less than 30 minutes. But Mary Jo, be a little gentler on Ken…he's not that short!

Keep up the great low-fat, healthy recipes. I enjoy the helpful hints, substitutions and alternate ideas…

Sincerely,

*Alfie*
Winnipeg, Man.

# 7-GRAIN BREAD WITH VEGETABLES, HERBS, GOAT CHEESE AND OLIVES

*Serves 4–6.*

Bread as a main dish for dinner is uncommon in North America.
Europeans, however, have been preparing variations of this for dinner
for hundreds of years. Experiment with various bread types and toppings.

| | |
|---|---|
| 6–8 slices | 7-grain bread |
| 3/4 lb | goat cheese, sliced |
| 1 | small zucchini, sliced lengthwise |
| 1 | small tomato, sliced |
| 1/2 cup | pitted black olives, sliced |
| 1 | sweet red pepper, sliced lengthwise |
| 1 cup | sliced mushrooms |
| 1 tbsp | chopped fresh rosemary |
| 1 tbsp | chopped fresh oregano |

Toast the bread. Arrange the vegetables on the toast
with the goat cheese. Sprinkle with herbs. Toast 4–5
minutes until cheese starts to turn golden.

**PREPARATION TIME:**     *15–25 minutes*

VARIATION:

For those who have wheat
allergies, use spelt or rice-
flour bread.

# STRIPED PITA VEGETABLES AND CHEESE

*Serves 4.*

| | |
|---|---|
| 4 | pita rounds |
| 1 cup | sliced green and red peppers |
| 1/2 | red onion, sliced |
| 1 cup | sliced carrot |
| 1/2 lb | Swiss cheese, sliced |
| 1/2 cup | chopped garlic chives |

Place the pitas on a baking dish. Layer the vegetables in a circle, evenly spaced; make it look colorful. Place cheese on top and grill on low for 15 minutes.

**PREPARATION TIME:**      *15–25 minutes*

# FOUR GOURMET PIZZAS

These gourmet pizza recipes are wonderful for getting your kids—or your friends—to help out in the kitchen. When prepared with the proper ingredients, pizza can be a truly healthy fast food. Keep in mind that these toppings can be mixed and matched; these are just suggestions.

**SEAFOOD DELIGHT:**
Shrimp, clams, smoked oysters, crab meat, cheddar

**VEGETARIAN PLUS:**
Onion, garlic, asparagus, sun-dried tomatoes, broccoli, oregano, feta

**MEAT LOVER'S HEAVEN:**
Pepperoni, sautéed ground beef, hot peppers, onion, mozzarella

**PIZZA À LA LOW FAT:**
Poached chicken, snow peas, ginger, red pepper, goat cheese

SUGGESTED SIDE DISH:
- Salad with mixed greens

**CRUST:**
Frozen pizza shells, or focaccia bread, or pita bread. Buy the pizza dough baked already, fresh from the supermarket. Or use your favorite homemade pizza crust.

**SAUCE:**

| | |
|---|---|
| 1 can | crushed tomatoes (28 oz/796 mL) |
| 2 tbsp | tomato paste |
| 1 clove | garlic |
| 1/4 cup | packed fresh basil (or 1 tsp dried) |
| 1/2 tsp | salt |
| 1/2 tsp | black pepper |

In a food processor, purée tomatoes, tomato paste, garlic, basil, salt and pepper. Build one of the suggested pizzas, or your own invention, and bake on a baking sheet at 375°F for 10 minutes.

**PREPARATION TIME:**    *15 minutes*

TIPS:

➤ Feta is a classic Greek cheese that is white and crumbly with a tangy, salty flavor. To remove some of the salt, soak the cheese in cold water or milk.

➤ Buy a part-skim mozzarella cheese.

➤ Microwaving chicken liquefies poultry fat so that it drains off. (Make sure to remove the skin, as it contains most of the fat.)

# EPILOGUE: AN APOLOGIA OF SORTS

By this point, you will have noticed that there is no dessert section. There are three reasons for this:

- it often takes longer than 30 minutes to bake or prepare a dessert

- I'm lactose-intolerant and most traditional desserts use dairy products

- I rarely eat desserts after meals, although I will on occasion treat myself to some fruit.

This said, for all those who crave sweets, I have been developing a variety of desserts for a future book, including some that are low-calorie and lactose-free. Please stay tuned!

# GLOSSARY

## TIPS

### EGGS

➤ Refrigerate eggs in their cartons so they don't absorb odors from other foods.

### FISH

➤ Cooking fish in foil retains the juices. The French use buttered paper in much the same way: this method is known as cooking en papillotte.

➤ Try to cook frozen seafood as soon as possible after purchasing. Avoid frozen fish with ice crystals, white patches or discoloration; all indicate freezer burn.

➤ Regulate your heat when cooking fish. Heat that is too high will cause the skin to break and the flesh to flake.

➤ Don't salt fish before grilling. Salt draws out the moisture of the fish and toughens it.

➤ Fish continues to cook after it is removed from the grill, so be careful not to overcook.

### FRUITS AND VEGETABLES

— Use bananas that are slightly green if you are going to broil, bake or sauté.

— Tomatoes will taste better if they are not refrigerated.

— Choose bunches of broccoli that are green throughout; yellow patches on florets denote age and toughness.

— Try to buy spinach in bundles, not bags; it will be fresher.

— Don't store potatoes and onions together, as the moisture in onions will cause potatoes to sprout.

— Keep onions refrigerated for "tearless" chopping.

— If roasting peppers (red or green), place them in a paper bag after roasting—this aids in the removal of skin.

— Eggplants don't keep very well; be sure to store them in the refrigerator, in a plastic bag.

## MEATS

➤ Choose the leanest blend of ground round, not ground chuck, which is higher in fat.

➤ Sliced turkey is one of the better cold cuts. It has little fat and is low in calories. But it is high in sodium, so look for a low-sodium brand.

➤ If grilling meat outside, add herbs to wood or coals for flavor. Jamaicans use this process to prepare "jerk" chicken or beef.

➤ Buy lamb on the bone, as it adds more flavor.

➤ When cooking sausages, poke holes in the skin to let the fat drain out.

➤ To minimize salt intake, avoid hams that are cured.

➤ The acids in citrus fruits are great for tenderizing meat.

## PASTA

➤ Uncooked pasta should be added gradually to a large quantity of rapidly boiling water. Cook pasta until tender; drain and rinse immediately in cold water.

## RICE AND GRAINS

➤ When cooking rice, add a tablespoon of oil or butter to the water to keep the grains from sticking together.

➤ Don't stir simmering rice; stirring makes the rice gummy.

➤ If the liquid evaporates before the rice is done, add a little more liquid and cook on low heat for a few minutes longer.

➤ Precook rice in the microwave.

➤ If not used frequently, store rice (especially brown rice) in the refrigerator to keep it fresh.

## SALADS

➤ Dry salad greens thoroughly, either in a salad spinner or with paper towels. Dressings will adhere better to the leaves, which means you will use less.

## SOUPS

- To remove excess fat from soup: let it chill so that fat solidifies then remove with a spoon.

- You can thicken soups with flour, potatoes, rice or bread crumbs.

- Garnish soups with minced herbs, chopped hard-boiled eggs, lemon slices, grated Parmesan, thin rounds of scallions, sour cream or yogurt.

- Leftover soups can be used as a base for pasta sauce, or in stir-fries and rice dishes.

- Freeze soups in one-serving containers to microwave later.

## STIR-FRIES

- You don't need a wok to stir-fry; just use an ordinary skillet with a lid.

- Add the thickest, toughest vegetables to the stir-fry first, and the most delicate last.

## TINS

- Don't buy canned food if the tin is dented, stained or bulging.

# COOKING STYLES TECHNIQUES AND TERMS

*Al Dente*

Pasta should be cooked al dente, which, in Italian, means "to the teeth," or until just done. Test doneness by biting into pasta; it should be tender but still firm.

*Antipasto*

Antipasto means "before pasta" in Italian; it is food served as an appetizer.

*Blanching*

Blanching is the technique of plunging fruit or vegetables into boiling water for a few minutes, and then removing and placing it in cold water to stop the cooking process. The purpose of blanching is to set the colour, or to partially cook and/or loosen the skin, making it easier to peel off.

*Bobotie*

Bobotie is a traditional Malay dish made of ground beef, curry, and fruit, which is also popular in South Africa.

*Coq au vin*

Coq au vin is simply chicken cooked in wine. Any good dry red wine will do. Burgundy is , however, the best choice.

*Fajitas*

Fajitas are grilled, marinated meat wrapped burrito-style in warm wheat- or corn-flour tortillas.

*Julienne*

Julienne means to cut vegetables into matchsticks or batons, approximately 3 inches in length.

*Hummus*

Hummus is a thick, Middle Eastern spread made from mashed chickpeas, tahini, lemon juice, olive oil and garlic.

*Mashed Potatoes*

For deluxe mashed potatoes, use mascarpone, a creamy Italian dessert cheese most often used in the dessert tiramisu.

Mashed potatoes are best served hot; to keep them warm, place in a pan over hot water.

*Perogies*

A perogie is a Polish pasta dumpling filled with mashed potatoes and cheese. For low-fat, low-cholesterol version, boil, rather than fry, the perogies. Traditionally, butter or sour cream is spread on perogies, but low-fat yogurt or salsa will do nicely as substitutes.

*Pita*

Pita is a versatile, Middle Eastern circular flatbread made of twice-risen dough that is baked a short time in a hot oven. The circles are separate though joined at the edges, and have a hollow centre. Pitas can be used as pizza crusts, cut into wedges and served with dip or sliced lengthwise to form two pockets, which can be filled. Whole wheat pitas offer more fiber.

*Poaching*

Poaching is a gentle method of cooking meat, fish or eggs in water or broth at a temperature just below that of simmering.

*Polenta*

Polenta is simply coarse cornmeal cooked with water and salt. But when sliced, coated in olive oil and grilled, it becomes a simple, delicious accompaniment to many dishes. It is sold in tubular form in most supermarkets; keep refrigerated.

*Primavera*

Primavera, Italian for "first green," actually refers to the first green vegetables of spring. Primavera sauce will include chopped carrots, zucchini, and so on.

*Reducing*

Boiling a sauce or liquid over high heat until it is reduced in volume, usually by half.

*Tapas*

Tapas means "appetizers" or "snacks" in Spanish. In Spain, tapas often replace dinner as a meal and will include a selection of small dishes such as mussels, clams, chicken, sausage, rice and vegetables.

*Tofu*

Tofu, which is made from soy beans, is an excellent source of vegetable protein. It can be sliced, diced or mashed and used in soups, stir-fries, casseroles and desserts. Tofu will keep for a week in a container of fresh water in the refrigerator; change water daily. Firmer pressed tofu is higher (by 34 percent) in vitamins and protein than tofu packaged in water.

*Zest*

"Zest" refers to the gratings from lemon, lime or orange rinds that are used to flavor dishes. Zest can be peeled or scraped by using a knife, or you can use a peeler or zester, both of which can be purchased in most kitchen stores.

## BASIC INGREDIENTS AND CONDIMENTS

*Almonds*

Almonds are a good source of fiber and are low in sodium. Toasting or dry-roasting almonds does not significantly alter their nutrient content.

*Brown Sugar*

Brown sugar is a combination of white sugar and molasses. Hardened brown sugar can be softened by placing an apple wedge in a plastic bag in the brown sugar container and sealing it tightly for a day or two.

## Dijon Mustard

Dijon mustard, originally from France, but now produced in both Canada and the United States, is made from husked and ground mustard seeds, white wine, vinegar and spices.

## Honey

The flavor of honey depends on the type of nectar collected by the bees. If honey crystallizes, just heat it in a microwave or place the jar in a bath of boiling water for a few minutes.

## Jalapeño Peppers

Jalapeño peppers are usually plump, the size of a thumb and have thick green skins. These are the most readily available of all the fresh chilies.

## Pine Nuts

Pine nuts, also called pignoli, are harvested from pine cones in Asia, particularly China, and are most famously used in the making of pesto. These nuts have a subtle, delicious flavor perfect for tossing into salads, pasta and rice dishes, or as garnish for soups. Because they have a high-fat content, they will only keep for a few months, if refrigerated.

## Salsa

Salsa is simply the Mexican word for sauce.

## Split Peas

Split peas are small green or yellow halved peas. You don't have to soak split peas before adding to a pot.

## Sour Cream

There are only 183 calories in one cup of low-fat sour cream.

## Soy Sauce

Soy sauce is high in sodium but low-sodium versions are available.

## Tahini

Tahini is a thick paste made of ground sesame seeds and is used to flavor Middle Eastern dishes such as hummus.

## Tamari

Tamari soy sauce is very high in sodium but it has a modest amount of calories and no fat. It has a stronger flavor than other soy sauces.

### Yogurt

Yogurt is the only high-quality source of protein derived from animals. It is an excellent source of calcium.

### Egg Substitutes

Egg substitutes are lower in both calories and fat than eggs, and contain no cholesterol. Use them instead of eggs in recipes that call for beaten, whole eggs.

# CHEESE

### Asiago

Asiago was originally made from sheep's milk but is now made from cow's milk. Aged asiago is preferable to young asiago, as the younger cheese tends to be more bitter.

### Blue Cheese

Blue cheeses are quite rich. Varieties include gorgonzola, stilton, and roquefort.

### Cheddar

Cheddar cheese can be white or orange, and its flavor can range from mild to sharp.

### Feta

Feta cheese is traditionally made from ewe's milk, but goat's milk and cow's milk are also used. The texture of feta can range from soft to semi dry but it is firm enough to hold its shape when sautéed or to crumble. Aged feta is salty and dry; soak in cold water to remove some of the salt.

### Gruyère

Gruyère is a nutty cheese that is only made in the summer from cow's milk.

### Parmesan

*Real* Parmesan cheese has "Parmigiano-Reggiano" etched on the surface of the rind: this denotes the region in Italy where Parmesan originated some seven hundred years ago.

It is best to buy Parmesan ungrated: if you need large quantities grated, use a food processor. Wrapped in foil and refrigerated, it will keep for weeks.

# FISH AND SHELLFISH

*Mussels*

Mussels should be alive, with their shells tightly closed. Avoid cracked or broken shells. And, like fish, mussels should never smell "fishy." Store mussels in cold water in the refrigerator. Use within one day of purchasing. (Cultivated mussels have less sand and grit.)

*Salmon*

Common varieties of salmon readily available are Atlantic, chum, king, pink, silver and sockeye.

*Scallops*

There are hundreds of species of scallops throughout the world; the two best known in North America are the large sea scallops and the smaller bay scallops.

Scallops should have a sweet, mild odor; strong-smelling scallops are not fresh. Refrigerate scallops in a leak-proof plastic bag in a bowl of ice. Cook scallops as soon as possible.

*Shrimp*

If you can, buy shrimp with the shell on as the shell protects the meat. Make sure the shells are shiny and firm. Black spots are a sign of age. Devein shrimp with a small pointed knife or toothpick. Cooked shrimp should be firm and white, with a very mild odor. If shrimp is tightly curled, it has been overcooked.

# FRUITS AND VEGETABLES

*Apples*

To prevent sliced apples from turning brown, sprinkle with lemon juice. For cooking, choose Golden Delicious or Granny Smith varieties.

Because apples continue to ripen once picked, store in perforated bags in the refrigerator and only rinse before eating.

*Apricots*

Apricots originated in China. It is said that Alexander the Great introduced them to Greece.

*Arugula*

Arugula is a tender, dark green lettuce with a peppery taste; the smaller leaves are the mildest.

## Asparagus

Asparagus is a member of the lily family and was a favorite of the French monarch Louis XIV. Asparagus is most abundant from April through June. Choose stalks with fresh, firm compact tips. When preparing asparagus, take each spear by its end and bend gently in half; it will snap approximately at the point where tenderness begins. Discard tough, woody ends (or use in soups).

## Butternut Squash

The club-shaped, buff-coloured butternut squash originated in Mexico and Central America.

## Carrots

Carrots are one of the best sources of vitamin A. Cooked carrots are easier to digest than raw ones; try steaming rather than boiling. Buy carrots with green tops; they are fresher than those without.

## Cauliflower

Cauliflower is high in fiber, vitamin C and carbohydrates.

## Cucumbers

Cucumbers belong to the melon family. Low in calories, they contain a small amount of fiber and no fat. Top cucumbers with a vinaigrette or low-fat yogurt for a side dish.

Cucumbers last for only three to five days because of their high water content. Store in a sealed plastic bag in the refrigerator.

## Cranberries

Cranberries are the only berries native to North America. They are a good source of vitamin C, and are low in fat and calories, if unsweetened. Fresh cranberries will keep for about a week, or you can freeze them for up to three months.

## Dates

Dates are very low in fat and sodium, and are a good source of potassium.

## Garlic

Garlic is a vegetable—it's a member of the lily family, as are onions, shallots, leeks and scallions. Garlic heads or bulbs should be large, firm and tight-skinned. Buy loose heads, which tend to be fresher than garlic packed in boxes. Store garlic in a cool, dry place—don't refrigerate.

An easy way to remove peel from garlic clove is to lay the flat of large knife on top and smash it with your palm; this loosens the peel, which can then be easily picked off.

### Leeks

Leeks—the national emblem of Wales—roughly resemble oversized scallions, but have a milder taste.

### Lettuce

The darker the lettuce leaves, the higher the vitamin A content.

### Lemons

To get the most juice from a lemon, make sure it's at room temperature before squeezing (if not, microwave on high for about 30 seconds). A single teaspoon of lemon juice contains 12 percent of your daily vitamin C requirement.

If a recipe calls for both lemon juice and lemon zest, grate the zest from the lemon first, then pour the lemon juice over the zest to keep it moist. Lemon juice and zest freeze well.

### Mushrooms

Mushrooms contain respectable amounts of fiber and complex carbohydrates, along with vitamin C.

Store mushrooms in the refrigerator, either in a paper bag or in an open container, covered loosely with a slightly damp paper towel. To keep mushrooms white, wipe them with water mixed with a little lemon juice.

### Olives

Kalamata olives are considered superior olives; the smallest of them have the most flavor.

Black olives are mature green olives that get their color either naturally from ripening on a tree or chemically from curing. While not exactly low in sodium, black olives have considerably less of it than green olives.

A popular misconception is that olives contain cholesterol; they do not, but they do contain iron.

### Oranges

A good seedless orange for cooking is the navel, which is large, thick-skinned and very sweet and juicy.

*Peaches*

Peaches are native to China; they came to Europe, and later to North America, through Persia—which explains the fruit's former name, persian apple.

*Pears*

Slightly underripe pears are best for cooking since they won't dissolve into mush. Pears are low in calories, fat and sodium, and are a good source of fiber.

*Plum Tomatoes*

Plum tomatoes are ideal for cooking as they have small seeds and little juice, and are rich in flavor.

*Potatoes*

Buy potatoes that are firm, smooth, well-shaped and heavy for their size. Potatoes that have a green tinge have been exposed to light—don't eat these, they will taste bitter and may make you sick (also discard any that are heavily sprouted). Microwaved potatoes retain their nutrients (such as vitamin C), unlike boiled potatoes. Leaving the skin on adds fiber to your diet. Potatoes have nearly twice as much potassium as bananas.

The best potatoes for mashing are mature ones, such as Yukon Golds, Idaho's and PEI varieties. Red potatoes are great for salads since they keep their shape and texture after boiling and when sliced and cubed (especially if you leave the skin on).

*Red Onion*

The red (or purple) onion originated in Italy. Raw red onions, as well as Bermuda and Spanish onions, are perfect chopped or sliced and tossed in salads, as they are sweet and mild-flavored.

*Red Peppers*

Red peppers are high in vitamin C, and a half cup of chopped raw red pepper has only 14 calories.

*Scallions*

Scallions, or green onions, are long, thin and green with white bulbs, and are sold in bunches. Scallions contain more nutrients than onions or leeks. The white bulb is a little stronger than the green stalks. Slice and use as a garnish, raw, in salads or on top of cooked dishes.

*Shallots*

The shallot is best described as a cross between a garlic and an onion.

*Spinach*

Frozen spinach is a good alternative to fresh, for cooking.

*Strawberries*

Strawberries are super-low in calories, fat and sodium, and are brimming with vitamin C.

*Sweet Potatoes*

The sweet potato, or yam, is the most nutritious vegetable on the planet.

*Yellow Tomatoes*

Yellow tomatoes are milder and less flavorful than their red counterparts but add lovely color to any dish.

*Zucchini*

Zucchini is a summer squash characterized by its thin skin, which is edible. It is high in vitamin A and one of the lowest-calorie vegetables.

## GRAINS AND PASTA

*Couscous*

Couscous is a staple of North African countries such as Morocco, Algeria and Tunisia. It is a low-fat, low-sodium semolina grain that makes an excellent substitute for rice. It cooks in roughly 5 minutes.

*Pasta*

Fresh pasta is lighter and richer than dried pasta. Fresh pasta is also more likely to contain egg than dried pasta. Refrigerated, fresh pasta keeps for about a week; frozen, it keeps for two to three months.

Egg noodles are both low in fat and a good source of fiber, but contain cholesterol.

*Rice*

There are three categories of rice: long-, medium- and short-grain. Long-grain is good for soups and pilafs. Medium- and short-grain rice—which tend to stick together when cooked—are good for puddings, rice rings and risottos.

*Wild Rice*

Wild rice has a nutty flavor and a chewy texture. It can contain sandy particles, and so needs careful washing. Wild rice takes longer to cook than both white or brown rice.

## HERBS AND SPICES

*Basil*

In Italy, basil—a member of the mint family—has always been a token of love. To preserve the taste of fresh basil, pack the fresh leaves, washed and well-dried, into a jar. Cover with olive oil, tightly cap and refrigerate. Refrigerated, it will keep for six months.

*Capers*

Capers are the unopened bud of a shrub that grows wild throughout the Mediterranean, North Africa and India.

*Cayenne Pepper*

Cayenne pepper is a dried, crushed hot spice named after the capital city of French Guyana.

*Chives*

Chives are slender grass-like herbs. Never cook chives: they are too delicate to stand up to heat. Instead, chop and use as a garnish.

*Coriander*

Coriander, also known as cilantro or Chinese parsley, is used to garnish and enhance many Thai dishes. It is often mistaken for Italian or flat-leafed parsley, although the taste is quite distinctive.

*Dill*

Dill, a member of the parsley family, was first "discovered" in England in 1597. The name dill comes from the Saxon word "dillan," which means "to lull." It was given to babies to help them sleep. Dried dill is often labeled dillweed.

*Ginger*

Powdered ginger is spicy and intense, with a slightly musty flavor, while fresh ginger root is sweet and tangy. Store fresh ginger in a lightly dampened plastic container with a tight-fitting lid in the refrigerator. It should keep for about a week.

### Mint

Of the more than thirty varieties of mint available, peppermint and spearmint are the best known; however, there are also lemon mint, orange mint and apple mint.

Mint sauce is easily made with fresh mint, a little vinegar and sugar to taste.

### Paprika

Paprika is ground from dried sweet red peppers. It is available in sweet, moderately hot and hot varieties.

### Parsley

Parsley is native to the Mediterranean and is a very nutritious garnish; it contains vitamin C, vitamin A and iron. There are two common varieties of parsley: the Italian flat-leaf, which has a stronger flavor, and the curly-leaf, which is perfect for garnishing.

Slightly wilted parsley can be revived in cold water.

### Rosemary

If you grow the herb rosemary in your garden, pick it when it flowers. Finely chop both the leaves and flowers, place in jars and cover with olive oil (if you do this, it must be stored in the refrigerator). The flavor of the herb is best released by mincing or crushing it in your hands.

# MEATS

### Bacon

Although bacon is high in fat, it does contain some B vitamins and vitamin C. Microwaving bacon and draining on paper towel is a good way to get rid of excess fat.

### Beef

Good cuts of beef for stewing are chuck, rump and round. To keep fat and cholesterol levels down, limit yourself to a 30-oz. serving of beef and trim excess fat. If using a less expensive cut of beef, marinate all day to ensure tenderness.

### Lamb

Lamb chops can be bought in different widths; thicker lamb chops are considered more flavorful than thinner. (If you leave the fat on the chop, the flavor will also be enhanced.) Rosemary is considered the classic herbal accompaniment to lamb; also try fresh mint, parsley, sage, thyme or basil.

*Pork*

Canadian pork is the leanest in the world and is prized on the international markets. Pork tenderloin has generous amounts of vitamin B and less fat than chicken with its skin on.

*Roasting Chickens*

Roasting chickens are about 10 weeks old and weigh between 4-1/2 and 8 lb., with more meat per lb than smaller birds.

*Sausage*

Sausage meat will keep for about two days in the refrigerator; it will keep for several weeks in the freezer, but the flavor will gradually deteriorate.

# OILS AND VINEGARS

*Balsamic Vinegar*

Balsamic vinegar is made from the unfermented juice of the white Trebbiano grape.

*Olive Oil*

The highest-quality olive oils are labeled "extra virgin" (which means they come from the first pressing of the olives and are, therefore, the finest), "superfine virgin," "fine virgin" and "virgin." Lesser-quality olive oils are labeled "pure" or just "olive oil"—these are much less flavorful than the virgin oils but more suitable for cooking.

The more expensive olive oils, such as extra virgin, are best used in salads, drizzled over vegetables or in place of butter on bread. Buy olive oil in small bottles and store away from heat and light.

*Rice Vinegar*

Rice vinegars are made in both China and Japan. This white vinegar has a sharp, clean taste that is somewhat mellower than distilled white vinegar.

*Sesame Oil*

Sesame oil is a light-coloured, nutty-flavored oil that is great for cooking. Don't confuse it with the dark-coloured, strongly flavored Asian sesame oil, which is not a cooking oil.

# INDEX

If you'd like to write to Ken Kostick, please address your letters to:

Ken Kostick

Box 116

2255 Queen Street East

Toronto, Ontario

M4E 1G3

# ABOUT THE AUTHOR

Born in Winnipeg, Toronto-based Ken Kostick
has had a varied career in travel and fashion,
including starting up his own modeling agency.
Most recently, he was hired by the Milan-based
agency, Flash, to act as an international model
scout. In this capacity, he logs thousands of
miles each year interviewing the most
beautiful young women in each city
he visits. Three years ago, Ken
began collecting recipes in
between searches for the next
supermodel. The result has
been the creation of the
*What's for Dinner?*
TV show and, now,
this cookbook.

photo by: George Nanos